DECORATED

Sublimely

Crafted Cakes

FOR EVERY

OCCASION

DECORATED

Sublimely

Crafted Cakes

FOR EVERY

OCCASION

APRIL CARTER

Photography by Danielle Wood

hardie grant books

MELBOURNE · LONDON

CONTENTS

INTRODUCTION

Can you imagine a birthday party, a wedding or even an afternoon tea without cake? For me, apart from the chance to satisfy my sweet tooth, a beautiful, thoughtfully crafted and delicious cake makes an occasion special, brings people together and makes them happy. I love that moment when the candles are blown out, the cake is cut, the slices are passed around and everyone gathers together to eat. All the better if you are the proud baker that made it happen.

Baking and decorating is such a creative process. When I'm planning a cake I think about the combinations of flavour and texture, the season, who the cake is for, how many people are going to be eating it and how I'm going to get it to its destination in one piece. Then, of course, I think about how it will be decorated. How do I hint at the flavours inside and make the cake look as delicious as it tastes? What look do I want to go for; casual and rustic, simple and elegant or maybe sparkly and glamorous? Sometimes I'll be keen to use a new technique that I've been meaning to try. More often than not I won't have much time so I'll go for one of my fail-safe recipes and a decorating technique that has maximum impact but is quick and easy to do.

Even confident bakers can be nervous about the decorating part of making a cake. In this book I have included some of my favourite flavour combinations and decorating ideas to inspire you, and step-by-step photographs with lots of hints and tips on how to achieve each look. When it comes to food, I prefer a simple approach and one of my favourite ways to create some drama and make a cake look special is

by adding height with lots of layers. Learning how to create perfectly even layers, smooth buttercream or confidently piped ganache can really step up the look of your cake and show off your baking skills. If you have zero time, just a sprinkling of icing (confectioners') sugar and a cluster of pretty candles can make a real difference too.

Once you've got the basics, you can have fun creating different looks and flavour combinations. The chocolate glaze from the Chestnut and Pear Cheesecake (see page 103) would work beautifully on the Burnt Butter Hazelnut Cake (see page 57). It would be fun to try a citrus version of the White Rose Cake (see page 98) with a pale lemon yellow and orange colour palette instead of the pink rose look. Make a Red Velvet and Raspberry Layer Cake (see page 84) version of the Stacked Victoria Sandwich (see page 51) or switch the pistachio cream in the Pistachio Choux Buns (see page 74) for an amaretto version topped with toasted almonds.

Delicious cakes get eaten quickly so remember to document your creations. I've included some of my tips for taking better photos of cakes towards the end of this book, even if it's just a quick snap on your phone.

So whether you're making something simple and tasty like the Carrot, Orange and Golden Pecan Cake (see page 64) or something grand like the Dark Chocolate and Blackberry Cake (see page 60), set some time aside to enjoy the creative process and have fun decorating!

BAKING TIPS

Baking and decorating a beautiful and delicious cake takes a bit of time and effort so it's worth starting with really good quality ingredients to get the best results possible. All of the recipes in this book use the following (unless otherwise stated):

- medium (large US) free-range eggs
- unsalted butter
- whole (full fat) milk
- unsweetened cocoa powder
- dark chocolate with 70 per cent minimum cocoa solids
- vanilla extract, not (often artificial tasting) essence

Make sure that all of your ingredients are at room temperature. This means taking your butter, eggs and milk out of the fridge for at least an hour before you start. Butter should be soft but still holding its shape (not melted or greasy). If you're in a rush, you can speed things along by cutting your butter into cubes and placing your eggs into some warm water. When everything is at room temperature you'll find it's much easier to cream your butter and sugar to incorporate air and your batter is less likely to curdle.

Successful baking relies on a careful balance between ingredients so it's worth measuring everything accurately. I always use electric scales for weighing out ingredients and proper measuring spoons for measuring tablespoons and one, half and quarter teaspoons. You can measure liquid ingredients like water and milk by weight too. If a recipe says '150 ml (5 fl oz) milk', simply weigh out 150 g (5 oz).

If you find that your cake batter curdles after you've added the egg or liquid ingredients, don't worry. Adding a tablespoon of your weighed out flour will help to bring it back together.

For a light-textured cake, it makes a difference if you cream your butter and sugar for at least 3–4 minutes using a stand mixer or electric hand mixer. I usually time myself to make sure that this step isn't rushed.

Once you have added the flour to your cake batter, don't be tempted to beat it in more than you need to, as this can make the cake tough (the liquid in the cake batter starts to develop gluten in the flour which is a good thing for bread but not for cakes).

When you have combined all of your ingredients, get the cake batter into the oven as quickly as possible to avoid large bubbles from forming (the raising agent will have started to work).

If you're baking a cake with multiple layers, weigh your cake batter into the cake tins to make sure that it's evenly distributed (this will make perfectly even layers) and – if possible – place both tins on the same oven shelf.

Before your cake goes into the oven, make sure that the shelves are in the right position and that the temperature is correct. Ovens vary but you can buy an inexpensive oven thermometer to check the temperature of yours. If you don't have a fan assisted oven, the middle shelf is best. Fan assisted ovens tend to have a uniform temperature across each shelf.

Avoid opening the oven door to check on your cake during baking, especially during the first 20 minutes, and try to get into the habit of writing down what time your cake went in or setting a timer. As ovens vary, check to see whether your cake is done 5 minutes before the cooking time is up. Most cakes are baked once they are springy to the touch and a skewer inserted into the centre of the cake comes out clean. Be careful not to bake for longer than you need to as this can dry cakes out. If your oven is too hot you can end up with a very domed or burnt cake and if it's not hot enough your cake could collapse.

Always let your cakes cool completely on a wire rack before splitting, decorating and storing them. Ideally, move the cake away from the oven to a cooler part of the kitchen.

ESSENTIAL EQUIPMENT

Here are my essential tools and equipment for successful and stress-free baking:

STAND MIXER OR ELECTRIC HAND MIXER – essential for achieving light cakes and pale, creamy buttercream. I have a KitchenAid stand mixer. It's a big investment but if you do lots of baking, it makes life so much easier as you can get on with other tasks while it mixes.

OVEN THERMOMETER – useful for making sure that your oven is at the correct temperature before baking.

TIMER – I always set a timer as soon as a cake goes into the oven so that there's no risk of forgetting about it.

MIXING BOWLS IN DIFFERENT SIZES – I have stackable heatproof glass bowls that are easy to store and can be used for melting chocolate and whipping up cake batters and buttercreams

CAKE TINS IN DIFFERENT SIZES – I have pairs of round deep (7.5 cm/3 inch) baking tins that are all the same make for uniform layers (they stack neatly inside each other so are easy to store), muffin tins for cupcakes and one or two bundt moulds. There are lots of speciality tins available but you can always bake a round or square cake and cut out shapes like hearts and letters once it has cooled instead of buying a particular shape of cake tin that you won't use again.

BAKING TRAYS – for toasting nuts and baking cookies.

WHISK – for whipping cream and combining ingredients.

SIEVE – to make sure that your dry ingredients are lump free and well combined.

RUBBER SPATULA – for scraping down mixing bowls to make sure that batters and buttercreams are evenly mixed. It's useful to get heatproof rubber spatulas so that you can use them for caramels too.

ROLLING PIN – for rolling out fondant icing (sugarpaste).

ELECTRIC SCALES – for accurately weighing out dry and liquid ingredients.

MEASURING SPOONS – for measuring quarter, half and full teaspoons and tablespoons

A MICROPLANE GRATER – you can make do without one of these but they are brilliant for grating citrus zest quickly and efficiently.

WIRE RACK – for even cooling.

DISPOSABLE PIPING BAGS – this means there's one less thing to clean up.

ICING TIPS – the ones that I use the most are plain round ones in two sizes, 8 mm (5/16 inch) and 12 mm (1/2 inch), an 8 mm (5/16 inch) large star tip (the Wilton 1M is good) and an 18 mm (3/4 inch) large star tip (try the Wilton 8D).

BAKING PARCHMENT – for lining cake tins. Also useful for wrapping and transporting cakes.

FOOD PROCESSOR – (with a blade attachment) useful for grinding nuts, but you can always use a pestle and mortar or the end of a rolling pin and a sturdy bowl if you don't have one.

A CAKE LEVELLER – for levelling and splitting your cakes. You can also use a good serrated knife if you don't have a cake leveller.

OFFSET AND STRAIGHT PALETTE KNIVES – good to have in two different sizes for spreading buttercream and ganache.

AN ICE-CREAM SCOOP – very handy for portioning out buttercream to get even layer cakes.

A CAKE TURNTABLE – you can get by without one of these but they are great for achieving a really smooth buttercream finish.

A SMALL PAINTBRUSH – for painting cakes with lustre dusts and gel food colouring.

A CHEF'S TORCH – not an essential item, but fun for finishing off toasted meringue icing.

GETTING ORGANISED

It's tempting to get going with baking your cake straight away but professional chefs always read the recipe through, weigh out their ingredients and prepare their tins before they start (known in kitchens as '*mise en place*' or getting 'everything in its place'). It's a much more efficient way of working and you can make sure that you have everything you need from the start so that nothing gets forgotten.

Try to plan your time and be realistic about how long it will take to get everything done, including the washing up, especially if you're baking and decorating a cake for a special event. I tend to be optimistic about timings and have had lots of late-night baking sessions over the years!

You can make the process easier and maximise your decorating time by doing as much in advance as possible, whether it's shopping for ingredients the day before or baking your cake layers ahead, wrapping them well and freezing them until they are needed. Most cakes taste best when they're freshly baked but will freeze well for a month. Just defrost the layers overnight at room temperature. You can also make things like fondant (sugarpaste) decorations, cake flags and chocolate curls well in advance.

Having a baking cupboard or box in your kitchen is a good way to keep all of your equipment and store cupboard ingredients together and organised, and it's easier to see when you've run out of something. I also keep a selection of birthday candles in a few different colours, some napkins, cake boards and boxes.

STORE CUPBOARD INGREDIENTS

Baking and decorating can be really spontaneous and creative, so it's good to have a few ingredients and supplies in your store cupboard for when you're feeling inspired. Don't be tempted to buy lots of everything though as all ingredients have a shelf life.

COCOA POWDER – not always easy to find in smaller local shops so it's worth keeping some in stock for short notice chocolate cakes. All of the recipes in this book use unsweetened cocoa powder.

DARK BROWN SOFT SUGAR – this gives a real depth of flavour to chocolate cakes and, unlike caster (superfine) sugar, isn't always available in local shops.

BAKING POWDER – if a recipe calls for self-raising flour, just add 4 teaspoons of baking powder to 225 g (8 oz) of plain (all-purpose) flour. Remember to check the date though as old baking powder may leave you with a cake that doesn't rise.

BICARBONATE OF SODA (BAKING SODA) – another useful raising agent and a key ingredient for making honeycomb.

DARK AND WHITE CHOCOLATE – so useful for ganache, chocolate buttercream and decorations (or to sneakily eat on its own!). I only ever bake with dark chocolate that has a high percentage of cocoa solids or white chocolate.

NUTS – I always have some walnuts, pecans, hazelnuts, pistachios or almonds in the cupboard as they lend flavour and texture to cakes as well as being useful to decorate with. Toast nuts in the oven to bring out their flavour.

SALT – Sweet and salty is definitely one of my favourite flavour combinations. I love how salt brings out the chocolate flavour in chocolate cakes and, of course, to use in salted caramel recipes.

SPICES – cinnamon is one of my favourite spices and goes with everything from apple to chocolate so I always have a supply. I also have nutmeg, cardamom, ground ginger and ground cloves to hand.

JAMS AND CURDS – I like to have these in the fridge to use as an easy filling for cakes (always good on crumpets and toast too).

EXTRACTS AND FLAVOURINGS – natural flavourings like vanilla extract (rather than essence) are best. I also like to keep rose water, orange blossom water and peppermint extract.

FONDANT (also known as sugarpaste or ready to roll icing) – for covering cakes and making decorations. Keep this well wrapped once it's been opened as it dries out easily.

GEL OR PASTE FOOD COLOURS – I keep a supply of basic colours that can be mixed to create other shades.

SPRINKLES – in a few different colours and shapes or make your own confetti sprinkles and store them in an airtight container (see pages 144–5). I also love shop-bought crystallised rose and violet petals and freeze-dried strawberries as an alternative to sprinkles.

WHITE NONPAREILS – tiny sprinkles that can also be coloured; just shake them in a small freezer bag with some lustre dust.

EDIBLE GLITTER AND LUSTRE DUST – this comes in lots of different colours but white is the best all-rounder. Match your glitter to the colour underneath (so red glitter for raspberries) for maximum impact. Lustre dust is a fine powder that can be used on its own or mixed with a little alcohol to form an edible paint.

ADAPTING RECIPES FOR DIFFERENT CAKE TINS

Cake tins can vary in width and depth and sometimes you might want to convert recipes depending on the equipment that you have and the look you're going for. All of the recipes in this book have been developed and tested in the tin sizes that the recipe calls for but it's worth experimenting by scaling recipes up and down.

Generally, you can double the quantities in a recipe to convert a 15 cm (6 inch) round cake to a 20 cm (8 inch) round cake. A 20 cm (8 inch) square tin will need around 20 per cent more cake batter to fill it than a 20 cm (8 inch) round tin. A recipe for 12 cupcakes can usually be baked in a single 20 cm (8 inch) round tin. If you're making a large layer cake in, say, a 25 cm (10 inch) round cake tin it's better to bake your cake in shallower layers as the middle might not bake correctly for deeper cakes.

Filling cake tins to a maximum of two thirds will ensure that your cakes bake evenly and don't overflow. A good way to compare your cake tin capacities is to measure how much water they can hold. For example, if your bundt tin and 20 cm (8 inch) round cake tin both have a capacity of 2 litres (3½ pints) you can be confident that if a recipe works in one, it will work in the other.

Keep in mind that the cooking time will vary depending on the size of your tins, so it's worth checking your cake a few minutes before you think it might be done. The oven temperature will stay the same.

PREPARING YOUR CAKE TINS

Always prepare your cake tins before you start mixing your ingredients. Once cake batter has been made, the raising agent will start working so it's best to get your cakes into the oven as soon as possible.

Draw around the base of your tin on to some silicone baking paper, or baking parchment and cut it out with scissors. Grease the base and sides of the tin with room-temperature butter on some baking paper or brush with melted butter or vegetable oil. Then you can position your paper base making sure that it fits the base of the tin exactly. Lining tins isn't always the most fun part of baking so I like to cut out a few circles in one go and keep them with my tins so that I always have a stash to use.

If you have a tin that is an unusual shape and can't be lined, like a bundt or tube tin, it's useful to buy a speciality product like 'cake release', which makes it really easy to get cakes out of their tins. Using plenty of butter usually does the trick though.

CHAPTER

1

The Cakes

|—————|

This chapter is a collection of recipes to inspire you but feel free to mix and match the flavour combinations and decorating ideas. From classics like Lemon and Poppy Seed Syrup Cake (see page 30) and new classics like Sea-Salted Caramel Chocolate Cake (see page 35) to cake alternatives like stacked up Pistachio Choux Buns (see page 74).

Simple Store Cupboard Chocolate Cake

This is my go-to recipe and everything you could want in a chocolate cake.
The sponge is moist and the brown sugar brings out the chocolate flavour beautifully.
It's really versatile too. I've halved the recipe to make a batch of 18 cupcakes before
and I've also doubled it to make a dramatic eight-layer wedding cake.

FOR THE CHOCOLATE CAKE:

110 g (3¾ oz/generous ¾ cup) cocoa powder
1½ teaspoons vanilla extract
260 g (9½ oz) unsalted butter
225 g (8 oz/1 cup) caster (superfine) sugar
225 g (8 oz/scant 2½ cups) soft dark brown sugar
6 medium eggs, lightly beaten
420 g (15 oz/3⅓ cups) plain (all-purpose) flour
4 teaspoons baking powder
1 teaspoon salt
270 ml (9½ fl oz) whole milk

FOR THE CHOCOLATE BUTTERCREAM:

375 g (13 oz) unsalted butter
520 g (1 lb 2 oz/generous 4 cups) icing (confectioners') sugar
120 g (4 oz/1 cup) cocoa powder
150 ml (5 fl oz) double (heavy) cream

TO DECORATE:

sparklers, candles, sprinkles or chocolate curls

EQUIPMENT | 2 x 18 cm (7 inch) round, deep cake tins | cake board or stand

PREHEAT the oven to 170°C (335°F/Gas 3). Grease the cake tins and line the bases with baking parchment. Place the cocoa powder, vanilla extract and 180 ml (6 fl oz) boiling water in a heatproof bowl and whisk to combine. Set aside to cool. In a clean bowl, using a stand mixer or electric hand mixer, beat the butter and sugars for 3–4 minutes, or until the mixture is pale and creamy. Add the beaten eggs to the butter mixture a little at a time, beating after each addition until they're well incorporated. Add the cooled cocoa mixture and beat well.

Sift the flour, baking powder and salt into a clean bowl. Add a third of the flour mixture to the butter mixture and beat until just combined. Add half of the milk, continuing to beat and scraping down the sides of the bowl as you go. Add another third of the flour, the remaining milk and the remaining flour and beat until just combined.

Divide the mixture evenly between the prepared cake tins. Bake in the oven for 50–60 minutes, or until a skewer inserted into the centre of each cake comes out clean. Allow the cakes to cool for 10 minutes in their tins, then turn them out onto a wire rack and leave to cool completely.

While the cakes are cooling, make the chocolate buttercream. Using a stand mixer or electric hand mixer, beat the butter in a bowl for 3–4 minutes until pale and creamy. Add the remaining ingredients and continue to beat for another 2–3 minutes until smooth.

Level the cakes by cutting off the domed tops and split each layer in half so that you have 4 layers in total (see pages 120–1). Fix the bottom layer of the cake to the cake board or stand with a small amount of buttercream. Spread the first layer with a generous amount of the chocolate buttercream. Place the second layer on top of this and repeat, and repeat again with the third layer, finishing with the final cake layer. Cover the cake with a thin layer of buttercream and chill for 30 minutes or until firm. Once firm, cover with the remaining buttercream (see pages 130–3). Decorate with a single sparkler, candles, sprinkles or chocolate curls.

Lavender Layer Cake

This is a laidback cake to serve with tea or some cloudy lemonade on a late summer's day.
I love the rustic tiered look but you could also bake this as a standard layer cake in two 18 cm (7 inch) tins.

FOR THE CAKE:
———

180 ml (6½ fl oz) whole milk
3 teaspoons dried lavender
180 g (6½ oz) unsalted butter
340 g (11½ oz/1½ cups) caster
(superfine) sugar
3 medium eggs, lightly beaten
260 g (9½ oz/generous 2 cups)
white spelt flour
1½ teaspoons baking powder
pinch of salt

FOR THE BUTTERCREAM:
———

90 g (3¼ oz) unsalted butter
140 g (5 oz/generous cup) icing
(confectioners') sugar
2 tablespoons double (heavy) cream
purple paste food colouring

TO DECORATE:
———

dried lavender
fresh flowers, pesticide free (see page 150)

EQUIPMENT | 15 cm (6 inch) round, deep cake tin
| 20 cm (8 inch) round, deep cake tin | cake board
or stand

POUR the milk and lavender in to a saucepan and gently heat to simmering for 2–3 minutes. Remove from the heat and set aside to cool. Once cool, strain through a sieve into a jug to remove the dried lavender.

Preheat the oven to 170°C (335°F/Gas 3). Grease the cake tins and line the bases with baking parchment. Using a stand mixer or electric hand mixer, beat the butter and sugar for 3–4 minutes or until pale and fluffy. Add the beaten eggs a little at a time, beating after each addition until they're well incorporated.

Sift the flour, baking powder and salt into a bowl. Add a third of the flour mixture to the butter mixture and beat until just combined. Pour in half the lavender-infused milk, continuing to beat, and then add a third of the flour mixture, the remaining milk and the remaining flour mixture and mix until combined. Spoon the same depth of mixture into the prepared tins. Bake in the oven for 35–40 minutes, or until a skewer inserted into the centre of each cake comes out clean. Allow the cakes to cool for 10 minutes in their tins, then turn them out on to a wire rack and leave to cool completely.

Make the buttercream. Use a stand mixer or electric hand mixer to beat the butter for 3–4 minutes until pale and creamy. Add the sugar and cream with a very small amount of purple paste food colouring and continue to beat for another 2–3 minutes until smooth.

Fix the 20 cm (8 inch) cake to a cake board or stand with a small amount of buttercream and spread the top with two thirds of the buttercream. Place the 15 cm (6 inch) cake on top, press down gently and spread the top with the remaining buttercream. Scatter over the dried lavender and decorate with fresh flowers.

Gingerbread Cake with Whiskey Caramel

The whiskey brings an oaky, smoky depth to the caramel in this cake and makes me imagine cosy winter nights in front of a log fire. The gingerbread layers are moist enough to eat on their own with a dusting of cinnamon icing sugar or served warm with vanilla ice cream and caramel sauce.

FOR THE CAKE:

225 g (8 oz) unsalted butter
110 g (3½ oz) black treacle
110 g (3½ oz) golden syrup
225 g (8 oz/scant 2½ cups) soft dark brown sugar
2 medium eggs
300 ml (10 fl oz) whole milk
350 g (12 oz/scant 3 cups) plain (all-purpose) flour
2 teaspoons bicarbonate of soda (baking soda)
4 teaspoons ground ginger
3 teaspoons ground cinnamon
pinch each of ground cloves, nutmeg and salt

FOR THE WHISKEY CARAMEL SAUCE:

250 g (9 oz/2½ cups) caster (superfine) sugar
300 ml (10 fl oz) double (heavy) cream
50 g (2 oz) unsalted butter
3–4 teaspoons whiskey
1–2 teaspoon flaky sea salt

FOR THE WHISKEY CARAMEL BUTTERCREAM:

300 g (10½ oz) unsalted butter
500 g (17¾ oz/4 cups) icing (confectioners') sugar
150 ml (5 fl oz) whiskey caramel sauce (see above)

TO DECORATE:

crystallised ginger, thinly sliced

EQUIPMENT | 2 x 18 cm (7 inch) round, deep cake tins | cake board or stand

PREHEAT the oven to 170°C (335°F/Gas 3). Grease the cake tins and line the bases with baking parchment. Heat the butter, treacle and golden syrup in a large saucepan over a low heat until the butter has melted. Beat in the sugar and set aside to cool slightly. Mix the eggs and milk together in a bowl to combine then slowly beat into the butter and sugar mixture. Sift the flour, bicarbonate of soda, ginger, cinnamon, cloves, nutmeg and salt into the saucepan and beat this until just combined.

Divide the mixture evenly between the prepared cake tins. Bake in the oven for 30–40 minutes, or until a skewer inserted into the centre of each cake comes out clean. Allow the cakes to cool for 10 minutes in their tins, then turn them out on to a wire rack and leave to cool completely.

While the cakes are cooling, make the whiskey caramel sauce and buttercream. To make the whiskey caramel sauce, heat the sugar in a large saucepan (a silver-coloured saucepan is best as you need to check the colour of the sugar as it melts) over a medium heat. Once the sugar starts to melt, swirl the sugar into the liquid areas of the pan without stirring. Meanwhile, gently warm the cream and butter in a separate pan until the butter has melted. After about 10 minutes, or once the sugar has completely melted and is dark amber in colour, remove the saucepan from the heat. Immediately whisk in the warm cream and butter mixture (be careful, as the hot caramel can splash up). If the sugar solidifies, return the pan to a medium heat

until the mixture is liquid again. Stir in the salt and the whiskey. Pour the mixture through a sieve into a heatproof bowl, to remove any lumps of sugar, and leave to cool.

To make the buttercream, using a stand mixer or electric hand mixer, beat the butter in a bowl for 3–4 minutes until pale and creamy. Add the icing sugar and whiskey caramel sauce and continue to beat for another 2–3 minutes until smooth.

Level the cakes by cutting off the domed tops and split each cake in half so that you have 4 layers in total (see pages 120–1). Fix the bottom layer of the cake to the cake board or stand with a small amount of buttercream. Spread the first layer with a generous amount of the whiskey caramel buttercream filling. Place the second layer on top of this and repeat, then repeat again with the third layer, finishing with the final cake layer. Cover the cake with a thin layer of buttercream and chill for 30 minutes or until firm. Cover with the remaining buttercream (see pages 130–3), chill for a further 10 minutes and pour over the rest of the whiskey caramel. If the caramel is too runny to set, chill for 10 minutes before pouring over the cake. Top with the crystallised ginger.

Lemon and Poppy Seed Syrup Cake

—I—

I make this refreshing cake on summer visits to the Czech Republic where poppy seeds are often used in baking. The bright yellow candied lemon slices can be made in advance or choose some yellow edible flowers to decorate.

FOR THE CANDIED LEMON:
———

2 unwaxed lemons
500 g (1 lb 2 oz/scant 2¼ cups) caster (superfine) sugar
500 ml (17 fl oz) water

FOR THE CAKE:
———

120 g (4 oz) unsalted butter
120 g (4 oz/generous ½ cup) caster (superfine) sugar
2 medium eggs, lightly beaten
120 g (4 oz/scant 1 cup) plain (all-purpose) flour
2 teaspoons baking powder
pinch of salt
2 tablespoons whole milk
20 g (¾ oz) poppy seeds
grated zest of 2 unwaxed lemons

FOR THE LEMON SYRUP:
———

juice of 1 lemon
125 g (4½ oz/generous ½ cup) caster (superfine) sugar

FOR THE LEMON DRIZZLE ICING:
———

125 g (4 ½ oz/1 ½ cups) icing (confectioners') sugar
juice of 1 lemon

TO DECORATE:
———

candied lemon (see above)
poppy seeds
edible flowers (see page 151)

EQUIPMENT | 20 cm (8 inch) round, deep cake tin

TO MAKE the candied lemon, slice each lemon into thin slices. Line a baking tray with baking parchment. Heat the sugar and water in a large saucepan over a medium heat until the sugar has dissolved. Once the sugar has dissolved, place the lemon slices into the saucepan in layers and cover with baking parchment to keep the lemon submerged. Simmer for 30 minutes, or until the lemon slices are translucent and the peel is tender. Transfer the slices to the lined baking tray and leave to cool and set for several hours, or overnight.

Preheat the oven to 170°C (335°F/Gas 3). Grease the cake tin and line the base with baking parchment. Using a stand mixer or electric hand mixer, beat the butter and sugar until the mixture is pale and fluffy. Add the beaten eggs a little at a time, beating after each addition until they're well incorporated. Sift the flour, baking powder and salt into a clean bowl. Add half of the flour mixture to the butter mixture and beat until just combined. Pour in the milk, continuing to beat, then add the remaining flour mixture and beat until just combined. Fold in the poppy seeds and lemon zest.

Pour the mixture into the prepared cake tin. Bake in the oven for 30–40 minutes, or until a skewer inserted into the centre of the cake comes out clean.

While the cake is baking, make the lemon syrup. Heat the lemon juice and sugar in a saucepan over a medium heat stirring occasionally until the sugar has dissolved. Use a skewer to make some holes in the just-baked cake, and pour over the syrup. Leave the cake to cool in the tin then remove and place on to a wire rack.

To make the lemon drizzle icing, mix the icing sugar with enough lemon juice to form a runny but opaque icing. Pour over the cooled cake and decorate with the candied lemon, poppy seeds and the edible flowers.

Sea-Salted Caramel Chocolate Cake

———

Chocolate and salted caramel have become an all-time favourite flavour pairing
for me. I've used sea salt in this cake so the cake flags are a nautical blue.

FOR THE CHOCOLATE CAKE:

110 g (3¾ oz/generous ¾ cup) cocoa powder
1½ teaspoons vanilla extract
260 g (9½ oz) unsalted butter
225 g (8 oz/1 cup) caster (superfine) sugar
225 g (8 oz/scant 2½ cups) soft dark brown sugar
6 medium eggs, lightly beaten
420 g (15 oz/3⅓ cups) plain (all-purpose) flour
4 teaspoons baking powder
1 teaspoon salt
270 ml (9½ fl oz) whole milk

FOR THE SALTED CARAMEL SAUCE:

375 g (13 oz/generous 3½ cups) caster (superfine) sugar
450 ml (15 fl oz) double (heavy) cream
75 g (2½ oz) unsalted butter
2–3 teaspoons flaky sea salt

FOR THE SALTED CARAMEL GANACHE:

400 g (14 oz) dark chocolate, finely chopped
400 ml (14 fl oz) salted caramel sauce (see above)

FOR THE SALTED CARAMEL BUTTERCREAM:

250 g (9 oz) unsalted butter
400 g (14 oz/3¼ cups) icing (confectioners') sugar
150 ml (5 fl oz) salted caramel sauce (see above)

TO DECORATE:

turquoise and white cake flags (see page 143)
flaky sea salt

EQUIPMENT | 2 x 15 cm (6 inch) round, deep cake tins | cake board or stand

PREHEAT the oven to 170°C (335°F/Gas 3). Grease the cake tins and line the bases with baking parchment. Place the cocoa powder, vanilla extract and 180 ml (6 fl oz) boiling water in a heatproof bowl and whisk to combine. Set aside to cool. In a clean bowl, using a stand mixer or electric hand mixer, beat the butter and sugars for 3–4 minutes, or until pale and creamy. Add the beaten eggs to the butter mixture a little at a time, beating well after each addition. Add the cooled cocoa mixture and beat well.

Sift the flour, baking powder and salt into a clean bowl. Add a third of the flour mixture to the butter mixture and beat until just combined. Add half of the milk, continuing to beat and scraping down the sides of the bowl as you go. Add another third of the flour, the remaining milk, then the remaining flour and beat until just combined.

Divide the mixture evenly between the prepared cake tins and bake in the oven for 50–60 minutes, or until a skewer inserted into the centre of each cake comes out clean. Allow the cakes to cool for 10 minutes in their tins, then turn them out on to a wire rack and leave to cool completely.

While the cakes are cooling, make the salted caramel sauce, ganache and buttercream. To make the salted caramel sauce, heat the sugar in a large saucepan (a silver-coloured saucepan is best as you need to check the colour of the sugar as it melts) over a medium heat. Once the sugar starts to melt, swirl the sugar into the liquid areas of the pan without stirring. Meanwhile, gently warm the cream and butter in a separate pan until the butter has melted. After about 10 minutes, or once the sugar is completely melted and dark amber in colour, remove the saucepan from the heat. Immediately whisk in the warm cream and butter mixture (be careful, as the hot caramel can splash up). If the sugar solidifies, return the pan to a medium heat until the mixture is liquid again. Stir in the salt. Pour the mixture through a sieve into a heatproof bowl, to remove any lumps of sugar, and leave to cool slightly.

For the ganache, place the chopped chocolate in a bowl and pour 400 ml (13 fl oz) of the warm caramel sauce over it. Gently whisk the mixture until it is completely smooth and all of the chocolate has melted. Transfer to a shallow container and set your chocolate mixture aside to cool, then chill for 20 minutes or until it is firm enough to spread.

To make the buttercream, using a stand mixer or electric hand mixer, beat the butter for 3–4 minutes until pale and creamy. Add the icing sugar and cool salted caramel sauce and continue to beat for another 2–3 minutes until smooth.

Level the cakes by cutting off the domed tops and split each cake in half so that you have 4 layers in total (see pages 120–1). Fix your first cake layer to the cake board or stand with a small amount of buttercream. Spread the first layer with a generous amount of the salted caramel buttercream filling and drizzle over 1 tablespoon of the salted caramel sauce. Place the second layer on top of this and repeat, then repeat again with the third layer, finishing with the final cake layer. Cover the cake with a thin layer of the remaining buttercream (see pages 130–3) and chill for 30 minutes or until firm.

Beat the ganache by hand until smooth then cover the cake with the ganache and decorate with sea-coloured cake flags and a sprinkling of flaky sea salt.

Chocolate, Orange and Cardamom Cake

Apart from being delicious on its own and fun to make, honeycomb can be
crumbled up or broken into shards and used as a dramatic cake decoration.

FOR THE CHOCOLATE CAKE:

75 g (2¹/₂ oz/generous ¹/₂ cup) cocoa powder
1 teaspoon vanilla extract
175 g (6 oz) unsalted butter
150 g (5 oz/²/₃ cup) caster (superfine) sugar
150 g (5 oz/generous 3/4 cup) soft dark brown sugar
4 medium eggs, lightly beaten
275 g (10 oz/2¹/4 cups) plain (all-purpose) flour
2¹/₂ teaspoons baking powder
¹/₂ teaspoon salt
10 green cardamom pods, seeds finely ground
180 ml (6¹/₂ fl oz) whole milk

FOR THE ORANGE BUTTERCREAM:

250 g (9 oz) unsalted butter
grated zest of one orange
400 g (14 oz/3¹/4 cups) icing (confectioners') sugar
100 ml (3¹/₂ fl oz) double (heavy) cream

FOR THE CARDAMOM HONEYCOMB SHARDS:

vegetable oil for greasing
250 g (9 oz/1 cup) caster (superfine) sugar
4 tablespoons clear honey
6 green cardamom pods, seeds finely ground
2 teaspoons bicarbonate of soda

EQUIPMENT | 2 x 15 cm (6 inch) round, deep cake tins | sugar thermometer
cake board or stand | piping bag fitted with an 18 mm (3/4 inch) large star tip

PREHEAT the oven to 170°C (335°F/Gas 3). Grease the cake tins and line the bases with baking parchment. Place the cocoa powder, vanilla extract and 120 ml (4 fl oz) boiling water in a bowl and whisk to combine. Set aside to cool. In a clean bowl, using a stand mixer or electric hand mixer, beat the butter and sugars for 3–4 minutes, or until the mixture is pale and creamy. Add the eggs to the butter mixture, a little at a time, beating well after each addition. Add the cooled cocoa mixture and beat well.

Sift the flour, baking powder, salt and ground cardamom seeds into a clean bowl. Add a third of the flour mixture to the butter mixture and beat, followed by half of the milk, scraping down the sides of the bowl as you go. Add another third of the flour, the remaining milk then the remaining flour and beat until just combined.

Divide the mixture evenly between the prepared tins and bake in the oven for 40–50 minutes, or until a skewer inserted into centre of each cake comes out clean. Allow the cakes to cool for 10 minutes in their tins, then turn them out onto a wire rack to cool completely.

While the cakes are baking and cooling, make the orange buttercream and the honeycomb. For the buttercream, using a stand mixer or electric hand mixer, beat the butter for 3–4 minutes until pale and creamy. Add the remaining ingredients and continue to beat for another 2–3 minutes until smooth. Cover the buttercream with cling film (plastic wrap) and store at room temperature until you're ready to use it.

For the honeycomb, lightly oil a 20 x 30 cm (8 x 12 inch) baking tin. Place the sugar, honey and 2 tablespoons of water in a large saucepan with a sugar thermometer attached. Gently stir over a medium heat until the sugar has dissolved. Once the sugar has dissolved, add the cardamom, stop stirring and increase the heat to 150°C (302°F). Remove from the heat and whisk in the bicarbonate of soda until just combined (be careful, it will bubble up). Immediately tip the mixture on to the prepared baking tin and leave to cool before breaking into shards.

Level the cakes by cutting off the domed tops and split each cake in half so that you have 4 layers in total (see pages 120–1). Fix your first cake layer to a cake board or cake stand with a small amount of buttercream. Spread the first layer with a generous amount of the orange buttercream. Place the second layer on top of this and repeat, and repeat again with the third layer, finishing with the final cake layer. Cover the cake with a thin layer of the buttercream and chill for 30 minutes or until firm. Once firm cover the cake with the remaining buttercream (see pages 130-3). To finish, pipe peaks using an 18 mm (3/4 inch) large star tip and decorate with shards of the honeycomb.

Toasted Porter, Peanut and Chocolate Cake

⊢━━━━⊣

The rich, dark flavour of London's porter beer pairs very well with the chocolate in
this cake and balances out the sweetness of the toasted meringue topping and the peanut
buttercream. If you can't find porter, you can use Guinness or any other stout.

FOR THE CAKE:

75 g (2½ oz/generous ½ cup) cocoa powder
300 ml (10 fl oz) porter or stout
225 g (8 oz) unsalted butter
350 g (12 oz/1½ cups) soft light brown sugar
4 medium eggs, lightly beaten
250 g (9 oz/2 cups) plain (all-purpose) flour
3 teaspoon baking powder
½ teaspoon salt

FOR THE PEANUT BUTTERCREAM:

120 g (4 oz) unsalted butter
150 g (5 oz/⅔ cup) icing (confectioners') sugar
2 teaspoons smooth peanut butter

FOR THE TOASTED MERINGUE ICING:

2 medium egg whites
100 g (3½ oz/½ cup) caster (superfine) sugar

EQUIPMENT | 2 x 15 cm (6 inch) round, deep cake tins | cake board or stand |
piping bag fitted with 1 cm (½ inch) plain tip | chef's blow torch

PREHEAT the oven to 170°C (335°F/Gas 3). Grease the cake tins and line the bases with baking parchment. Place the cocoa powder and porter in a bowl and whisk to combine. In a clean bowl, using a stand mixer or electric hand mixer, beat the butter and sugar for 3–4 minutes, or until the mixture is pale and creamy. Add the beaten eggs to the butter mixture a little at a time, beating after each addition until they're well incorporated.

Sift the flour, baking powder and salt into a clean bowl. Add half of the flour mixture to the butter mixture and beat, followed by the cocoa mixture, scraping down the sides of the bowl as you go. Finally, add the remaining flour and beat until just combined. Divide the mixture evenly between the prepared cake tins. Bake in the oven for 40–50 minutes, or until a skewer inserted into the centre of each cake comes out clean. Allow the cakes to cool for 10 minutes in their tins, then turn them out on to a wire rack and leave to cool completely.

While the cakes are cooling, make the peanut buttercream. Using a stand mixer or electric hand mixer, beat the butter for 3–4 minutes until pale and creamy. Add the remaining ingredients and continue to beat for another 2–3 minutes until the buttercream is smooth.

Level the cakes by cutting off the domed tops with a cake leveller or a serrated knife and split each cake in half so that you have 4 layers in total. Fix the bottom layer of the cake to the cake board or stand with a small amount of buttercream. Spread with one third of the buttercream. Place the second layer on top of this and repeat, then repeat again with the third layer, finishing with the final cake layer (see pages 130-1).

For the toasted meringue icing, place the egg whites in a clean, grease-free bowl. Using a stand mixer or electric hand mixer, whisk until stiff peaks form. Add 1 tablespoon of the caster sugar and whisk until stiff and glossy. Add another 2 tablespoons of caster sugar, whisking until stiff and glossy after each addition, then add the remaining sugar gradually, with the beaters still running, until the mixture is stiff and glossy and all of the sugar has been incorporated. Transfer the mixture to the piping bag and pipe on to the cake (see pages 134–7), toasting the top with a chef's blow torch to finish.

Chocolate-Chip Cookie Layer Cake

───┤─────├───

Chocolate-chip cookies are one of my favourite sweet treats and are so simple to make and quick to bake. This is a fun alternative to a layer cake, and is easy to transport to the pub or a friend's house for a birthday bite. As you can imagine, it's quite rich and you only need a thin slice so there's always enough to go round. If you're in a rush, skip the ganache and just pile the cookies up with a candle on top.

FOR THE COOKIE LAYERS:
───

125 g (4½ oz) unsalted butter
85 g (3 oz/⅓ cup) caster (superfine) sugar
125 g (4½ oz/⅔ cup) soft light brown sugar
1 medium egg, lightly beaten
175 g (6 oz) dark chocolate, roughly chopped
225 g (8 oz/scant 2 cups) plain (all-purpose) flour
1 teaspoon bicarbonate of soda (baking soda)
½ teaspoon sea salt

FOR THE CHOCOLATE GANACHE:
───

175 ml (6 fl oz) double (heavy) cream
200 g (7 oz) dark chocolate, finely chopped

USING a stand mixer or an electric hand mixer, beat the butter and sugars until the mixture is pale and fluffy. Add the beaten egg to the butter mixture a little at a time, mixing well to combine. Add the chopped chocolate.

Sift the flour, bicarbonate of soda and salt into a clean bowl. Gradually add the flour mixture to the butter mixture, beating until it is just combined. Cover the bowl and chill for at least 2 hours.

When your cookie dough is fully chilled, preheat the oven to 170°C (335°F/Gas 3). Line 2 baking trays with baking parchment. Divide the dough into 8 equal pieces (about 100 g/3 ½ oz each), roll into balls with your hands, press into thick disks and place on the baking trays 5 cm (2 inches) apart – the cookies will spread slightly as they bake. It should be possible to fit 2 cookies on each tray, so you will need to work in 2 batches. Bake in the oven for 10–12 minutes, or until just firm and golden at the edges. Leave the cookies to cool on the baking trays for 2–3 minutes before transferring the cookies, on the baking parchment, to fully cool on a wire rack. Repeat with the rest of the dough so that you have 8 cookies in total.

To make the chocolate ganache, heat the cream in a saucepan over a medium heat until small bubbles appear. Place the chopped chocolate in a bowl and pour the cream over it. Gently whisk the mixture until it is completely smooth and all of the chocolate has melted. Set your chocolate mixture aside to cool, then chill for 20 minutes or until it is firm enough to spread, then beat by hand until smooth.

To assemble, spread about 3 tablespoons of the chocolate ganache almost to the edge of the first cookie layer, press the second cookie layer on top and repeat until you have used up all of the cookies and ganache, finishing with a cookie layer. Wrap in cling film (plastic wrap) and chill for 30 minutes to set the ganache and soften the cookie layers. Serve at room temperature.

Stacked Victoria Sandwich

⊢━━━━━━⊣

This is a variation on the Simple Vanilla Cake on page 66 and, decorated with fresh flowers or fruit, it makes a beautiful and modern-looking wedding cake. It's best to eat this on the day it's baked but, as it takes a while to make, I've added a sugar syrup to keep the sponge moist. If you're making this for a special occasion, you can always freeze the layers, wrapping them well with cling film (plastic wrap) first, and defrost them overnight before filling them and stacking them up.

FOR THE 20 CM (8 INCH) CAKE TIER:

340 g (11½ oz) unsalted butter
450 g (1 lb/scant 2 cups) caster (superfine) sugar
6 medium eggs, lightly beaten
450 g (1 lb/3½ cups) plain (all-purpose) flour
4 teaspoons baking powder
½ teaspoon salt
2 teaspoons vanilla extract
180 ml (6½ fl oz) whole milk

FOR THE 15 CM (6 INCH) CAKE TIER:

225 g (8 oz) unsalted butter
300 g (10½ oz/scant 1⅓ cups) caster (superfine) sugar
4 medium eggs, lightly beaten
300 g (10½ oz/2½ cups) plain (all-purpose) flour
2½ teaspoons baking powder
¼ teaspoon salt
1 teaspoon vanilla extract
120 ml (4 fl oz) whole milk

Ingredients continued overleaf

110 g (3 ½ oz) unsalted butter
150 g (5 oz/⅔ cup) caster (superfine) sugar
2 medium eggs, lightly beaten
150 g (5 oz/1 ¼ cups) plain (all-purpose) flour
1 ½ teaspoons baking powder
pinch of salt
½ teaspoon vanilla extract
60 ml (2 fl oz) whole milk

FOR THE ELDERFLOWER OR VANILLA SUGAR SYRUP:

200 g (7 oz/generous ¾ cup) caster (superfine) sugar
200 ml (7 fl oz) water
4 tablespoons elderflower cordial (or 1 teaspoon vanilla extract)

FOR THE FILLING:

375 g (13 oz) unsalted butter
600 g (1 lb 3 oz/scant 5 cups) icing (confectioners') sugar
150 ml (5 fl oz) double (heavy) cream
2 teaspoons vanilla extract
250 g (9 oz) raspberry jam

TO DECORATE:

icing (confectioners') sugar for dusting
fresh fruit
fresh flowers, pesticide free (see page 150)

EQUIPMENT | 2 x 20 cm (8 inch) round, deep cake tins |
1 or 2 x 15 cm (6 inch) round, deep cake tin(s) | 1 or 2 x 10 cm (4 inch) round,
deep cake tin(s) | cake boards x 3 | cake dowels or plastic lolly sticks

PREHEAT the oven to 170°C (335°F/Gas 3). Grease the two 20 cm (8 inch) cake tins and line the bases with baking parchment. Using a stand mixer or electric hand mixer, beat the butter and sugar for the 20 cm (8 inch) tier for 3–4 minutes or until the mixture is pale and fluffy. Add the beaten eggs a little at a time, beating after each addition until they're well incorporated.

Sift the flour, baking powder and salt into a clean bowl. Add half of the flour mixture to the butter mixture and beat until just combined. Add the vanilla extract and milk, continuing to beat, and then add the remaining flour mixture and beat until just combined.

Divide the mixture evenly between the prepared cake tins. Bake in the oven for 45–50 minutes, or until a skewer inserted into the centre of each cake comes out clean. Allow the cakes to cool for 10 minutes in their tins, then turn them out onto a wire rack and leave to cool completely.

Repeat with the ingredients for the 15 cm (6 inch) and 10 cm (4 inch) cakes. I like to make the cake mixture for these in one batch, dividing it between the 4 tins so that they are level. If you only have one 10 cm (4 inch) and one 15 cm (6 inch) tin, make half of the total batch and split it between the 2 tins, then repeat.

To make the elderflower or vanilla sugar syrup, place the sugar and water in a saucepan and simmer gently, stirring occasionally, until the sugar has dissolved. Stir in the elderflower cordial or vanilla extract and set aside to cool.

To make the buttercream, using a stand mixer or electric hand mixer, beat the butter for 3–4 minutes until pale and creamy. Add the icing sugar, cream and vanilla extract, and continue to beat for another 2–3 minutes until smooth.

Level and split each cake so that each of the 3 tiers has 4 layers in total (see pages 120–1). Starting with the 20 cm (8 inch) tier, fix the bottom layer cut-side up on to a cake board with a small amount of buttercream. Brush with the sugar syrup and spread with buttercream, all the way to the sides. Place the next layer on top and press down evenly. Brush with sugar syrup, then spread with the raspberry jam. Add another layer of cake, sugar syrup and buttercream. Brush the cut side of the final layer with sugar syrup and place cut-side down to finish. Make sure that your layers are in line with each other and tidy up any buttercream that might have escaped by running your palette knife around the sides at a 45-degree angle. Repeat with the 15 cm (6 inch) and 10 cm (4 inch) layers.

Assemble the tiers (see pages 124–5), dust with icing sugar and decorate with the fresh fruit and flowers, using hidden cocktail sticks to keep everything in place.

Burnt Butter Hazelnut Cake

The burnt butter in this cake contributes to the nutty flavour of the toasted hazelnuts. Toasting nuts before baking with them is a great way to bring out their flavour. The rounded top that the bundt tin gives this cake is perfect for drizzling icing over and the pretty details mean that you don't need to do too much in the way of decorating.

FOR THE CAKE:

250 g (9 oz) unsalted butter
225 g (8 oz/scant 2½ cups) soft light brown sugar,
plus 2 tablespoons for grinding the nuts
125 g (4½ oz/scant cup) blanched hazelnuts
175 g (6 oz/scant 1½ cups) plain (all-purpose) flour
3½ teaspoons baking powder
¼ teaspoon salt
5 medium eggs
1 teaspoon vanilla extract

FOR THE CANDIED HAZELNUTS:

150 g (5 oz/⅔ cup) caster (superfine) sugar
300 ml (10 fl oz) water
50 g (2 oz/⅓ cup) blanched hazelnuts

FOR THE ICING:

250 g (9 oz/2 cups) icing (confectioners') sugar
2–3 tablespoons Frangelico hazelnut liqueur (optional)
25 g (1 oz) unsalted butter

EQUIPMENT | 20 cm (8 inch) bundt tin or round,
deep cake tin | sugar thermometer

PREHEAT the oven to 170°C (335°F/Gas 3) and grease the bundt or cake tin. Melt the butter over a medium heat and simmer until it turns a deep golden brown and starts to smell nutty. Pass the melted butter through a sieve into a clean bowl and stir in the sugar. Set aside to cool.

Spread the hazelnuts for the cake out on to a baking tray and bake in the oven for 5–8 minutes until golden brown. Set aside to cool slightly. Using a food processor, finely grind the hazelnuts with 2 tablespoons of the soft light brown sugar – avoid over-processing as the mixture will become greasy.

Sift the flour, baking powder and salt into a clean bowl. Add the eggs and vanilla extract to the cooled butter mixture and beat to combine. Gradually add the butter mixture to the flour mixture and beat until just combined. Finally, gently fold in the ground hazelnuts.

Spoon the mixture into the prepared tin and bake in the oven for 35–40 minutes, or until a skewer inserted into the centre of the cake comes out clean. Leave the oven on for the candied hazelnuts. Allow the cake to cool for 10 minutes in the tin, then turn it out on to a wire rack and leave to cool completely.

While the cake is cooling, make the candied hazelnuts and the icing. To make the candied hazelnuts, gently heat the sugar and water in a medium pan with a sugar thermometer attached and swirl until the sugar has dissolved. Increase the heat to 121°C (250°F) (this will take up to 10 minutes; remember to keep an eye on the temperature as it will increase quite quickly towards the end). Meanwhile, spread the hazelnuts out on to a baking tray and bake in the oven for 5–8 minutes until golden brown. Line another baking tray with baking parchment. As soon the sugar syrup has reached 121°C (250°F), turn off the heat and stir in the warm hazelnuts. Keep stirring until the clear syrup coats the nuts and turns crunchy and white. Tip the hazelnuts onto the prepared baking tray and separate with fork.

To make the icing, beat the icing sugar, hazelnut liqueur or 2–3 tablespoons of water and butter in a bowl until smooth. The icing should be opaque but thin enough to run down the sides of the cake.

To assemble the cake, beat the icing until smooth again. With the cake on the wire rack, drizzle a generous amount of icing over the top. Decorate with the candied hazelnuts and transfer to a cake stand or plate.

Dark Chocolate and Blackberry Cake

—|—

This beauty would make a chic evening centrepiece with its sparkling blackberries. It's quite a big cake so feel free to make a smaller one by halving the quantities.

FOR THE CHOCOLATE CAKE:

150 g (5 oz/1¼ cups) cocoa powder
2 teaspoons vanilla extract
350 g (12 oz) unsalted butter
300 g (10½ oz/scant 1⅓ cups) caster (superfine) sugar
300 g (10½ oz/1½ cups) soft dark brown sugar
8 medium eggs, lightly beaten
550 g (1 lb 3½ oz/scant 4½ cups) plain (all-purpose) flour
5 teaspoons baking powder
1 teaspoon salt
360 ml (11½ fl oz) whole milk

FOR THE CHOCOLATE GANACHE:

800 ml (27 fl oz) double (heavy) cream
800 g (1 lb 12 oz) dark chocolate, finely chopped

FOR THE BLACKBERRY MASCARPONE FILLING:

150 g (5 oz) fresh blackberries
2 tablespoons caster (superfine) sugar
1 teaspoon vanilla extract
400 g (14 oz/generous 1¾ cups) mascarpone
150 g (5 oz/1¼ cups) icing (confectioners') sugar

TO DECORATE:

225 g (8 oz) fresh blackberries
black edible glitter

EQUIPMENT | 2 x 13 cm (5 inch) round, deep cake tins | 2 x 18 cm (7 inch) round, deep cake tins | piping bag | cake boards x 2

PREHEAT the oven to 170°C (335°F/Gas 3). Grease the cake tins and line the bases with baking parchment. Place the cocoa powder, vanilla extract and 240 ml (8½ fl oz) boiling water in a heatproof bowl and whisk to combine. Set aside to cool. In a clean bowl, using a stand mixer or electric hand mixer, beat the butter and sugars for 3–4 minutes, or until the mixture is pale and creamy. Add the beaten eggs to the butter mixture a little at a time, beating well after each addition. Add the cooled cocoa mixture and beat well.

Sift the flour, baking powder and salt into a clean bowl. Add a third of the flour mixture to the butter mixture and beat until just combined. Add half of the milk, continuing to beat, scraping down the sides of the bowl as you go. Add another third of the flour mixture, the remaining milk followed by the remaining flour and beat until just combined.

Divide the mixture evenly between the 4 prepared tins. Bake in the oven for 40–50 minutes, or until a skewer inserted into the centre of each cake comes out clean (the smaller cakes might be ready a few minutes before the larger ones). Allow the cakes to cool for 10 minutes in their tins before turning them out on to a wire rack to cool completely.

While the cakes are cooling, make the chocolate ganache and blackberry mascarpone filling. For the ganache, heat the cream in a saucepan over a medium heat until small bubbles appear (scalding point). Place the chopped chocolate in a bowl and pour the cream over it. Gently whisk the mixture until it is completely smooth and all of the chocolate has melted. Set your

chocolate mixture aside to cool, then chill for about 20 minutes or until it is firm enough to use for ganache, then beat by hand until smooth. For the mascarpone filling, place the blackberries, caster sugar and vanilla extract in a bowl and lightly crush the berries with the back of a fork as you combine the mixture. In a clean bowl, beat the mascarpone and icing sugar by hand until smooth. Fold in the crushed blackberry mixture until just combined, leaving a ripple effect.

Level the cakes by cutting off the domed tops and split each cake in half so that you have 8 layers in total (see pages 120–1). Fill a piping bag with the ganache and snip off the end (see page 134–5). Fix the first layer of the larger cake to a cake board with a small amount of ganache. Pipe some ganache around the edge of the first layer and fill with some of the marscarpone filling (see pages 122–3). The ganache stops the mascarpone filling from escaping. Place the second layer on top of this, add the ganache and mascapone as you did with the first layer, repeat with the third layer, finishing with the fourth cake layer. Repeat with the smaller cake so that you have 2 cake tiers, each sitting on a cake board. Cover both of the cake tiers with a thin layer of the chocolate ganache and chill for 30 minutes or until firm. Meanwhile, for the decoration, dip the blackberries into the black glitter (see page 148).

Assemble the tiers (see page 124–5), then cover the cake with the remaining ganache and decorate with the glittered blackberries. You can use hidden cocktail sticks to stop the blackberries from falling off the cake.

Carrot, Orange and Golden Pecan Cake

This is a classic daytime cake with orange zest through the not-too-sweet mascarpone
to keep things fresh, and golden pecans for a bit of glamour.

FOR THE CAKE:

100 g (3½ oz/1 cup) pecans
170 g (6 oz/¾ cup) caster (superfine) sugar
150 g (5 oz/generous ¾ cup)
soft dark brown sugar
180 ml (6½ fl oz) vegetable oil
3 medium eggs
225 g (8 oz/scant 2 cups)
plain (all-purpose) flour
1½ teaspoons baking powder
1½ teaspoons bicarbonate of soda
3 teaspoons ground cinnamon
pinch of salt
200 g (7 oz) peeled and coarsely grated
carrot (about 6 medium carrots)
grated zest of half an orange

FOR THE GOLDEN PECAN DECORATION:

50 g (2 oz/½ cup) pecans
gold lustre dust
2–3 drops of rejuvenator spirit or vodka

FOR THE ORANGE MASCARPONE ICING:

250 g (9 oz/generous cup) mascarpone
grated zest of half an orange
75 g (2½ oz/scant ⅔ cup)
icing (confectioners') sugar

EQUIPMENT | 20 cm (8 inch) deep, round cake tin

PREHEAT the oven to 170°C (335°F/Gas 3).
Grease the cake tin and line the base with baking
parchment. Spread the pecans for the cake and the
decoration on to a baking tray and bake in the oven
for 5–8 minutes until golden brown and aromatic.
Set aside to cool slightly, saving 50 g (2 oz) for the
decoration. Roughly chop 100 g (3½ oz) of the
pecans to use in the cake. Using a stand mixer or
electric hand mixer, beat the sugars, oil and eggs in
a large bowl until pale.

Sift the flour, baking powder, bicarbonate of
soda, cinnamon and salt into a clean bowl. Add the
flour mixture to the sugar, oil and egg mixture
and beat until just combined. Finally, fold in the
grated carrot, orange zest and chopped pecans.

Spoon the mixture into the prepared cake tin.
Bake in the oven for 50–60 minutes, or until
a skewer inserted into the centre of the cake comes
out clean. Allow the cake to cool for 10 minutes in
the tin, then turn it out on to a wire rack and leave
to cool completely.

While the cake is cooling, make the icing and
golden pecans. To make the golden pecans, mix a
little of the gold lustre dust in a small bowl with
a few drops of rejuvenator spirit or vodka to form
a paste. Use a clean paint brush to paint your
pecans (see page 147). To make the icing, place
the mascarpone and orange zest in a bowl and
beat until smooth. Add the icing sugar and beat
again until smooth. Spread over the top of the
cooled cake and decorate with the golden pecans.

Simple Vanilla Cake, Four Ways

⊢————⊣

Everyone needs a classic vanilla cake in their recipe repertoire. This one is delicious, buttery and tender. To show off its versatility, I've decorated the cake four ways so that once you've got the baking part done you can dust it with icing sugar or go all out with buttercream and sprinkles.

FOR THE CAKE:

225 g (8 oz) unsalted butter
300 g (10½ oz/scant 1⅓ cups) caster (superfine) sugar
4 medium eggs, lightly beaten
300 g (10½ oz/2½ cups) plain (all-purpose) flour
2½ teaspoons baking powder
¼ teaspoon salt
120 ml (4 fl oz) whole milk
1 teaspoon vanilla extract

FOR THE FILLING:

4½ tablespoons raspberry jam

FOR THE VANILLA BUTTERCREAM (IF USING):

200 g (7 oz) unsalted butter
320 g (11 oz/generous 2½ cups) icing (confectioners') sugar
80 ml (3 fl oz) double (heavy) cream
1 teaspoon vanilla extract

1

FOR THE 'AFTERNOON TEA' LOOK:

—

icing (confectioners') sugar, to dust

2

FOR THE 'SUMMER BERRIES AND CREAM' LOOK:

—

1–2 tablespoons icing (confectioners') sugar, plus extra for dusting
150 ml (5 fl oz) double (heavy) cream
handful of fresh strawberries, raspberries,
redcurrants or any seasonal berries

3

FOR THE 'GROWN-UP PARTY' LOOK:

—

vanilla buttercream
lots of birthday candles

4

FOR THE 'CHILDREN'S PARTY' LOOK:

—

vanilla buttercream
sprinkles
number birthday candle

EQUIPMENT | 2 x 13 cm (5 inch) round, deep cake tins | cake board or stand

PREHEAT the oven to 170°C (335°F/Gas 3) and grease and line the cake tins. Using a stand mixer or electric hand mixer, beat the butter and sugar for 3–4 minutes or until the mixture is pale and fluffy. Add the beaten eggs a little at a time, beating after each addition until they're well incorporated. If the mixture curdles add a tablespoon of flour to bring it back together.

Sift the flour, baking powder and salt into a clean bowl. Add half of the flour mixture to the butter mixture and beat until just combined. Add the milk and vanilla extract, continuing to beat, and then add the remaining flour mixture and beat until just combined.

Divide the mixture evenly between the prepared cake tins. Bake in the oven for 35–40 minutes, or until a skewer inserted into the centre of each cake comes out clean. Allow the cakes to cool for 10 minutes in their tins, then turn them out on to a wire rack to cool completely. Level the cakes with a cake leveller or a serrated knife and split each cake in half, making 4 layers (see pages 120–1). Fix the bottom layer to the cake board or stand with a teaspoon of jam or buttercream.

FOR 1: Fill each layer with 1–2 tablespoons of jam and dust the top of the cake with icing sugar.
FOR 2: Add the icing sugar to the cream and whisk until it just holds its shape. Top the cake with the cream and berries, dust with icing sugar and serve.
FOR 3: Make the vanilla buttercream (see page 54). Crumb coat and smoothly ice the cake (see pages 130–3). Decorate with candles.
FOR 4: Follow the steps in version 3, then decorate the iced cake with sprinkles and top with a single candle.

Black Forest Torte

This tower of boozy cherries, cocoa cream and layers of chocolate cake is an indulgent but minimal update to the classic. Poaching the fresh cherries in sugar syrup and kirsch really brings out their flavour. I've named this cake a 'torte' in honour of its German roots.

FOR THE CAKE:

80 g (2¾ oz) unsalted butter
190 g (6⅔ oz/generous ⅓ cup) caster (superfine) sugar
6 medium eggs
120 g (4 oz/1 cup) plain (all-purpose) flour
70 g (2¼ oz/generous ½ cup) cocoa powder

FOR THE KIRSCH-POACHED CHERRIES:

120 g (4 oz/generous ½ cup) caster (superfine) sugar
6 tablespoons kirsch
450 g (1 lb) fresh cherries, halved, stones removed

FOR THE CREAM FILLING:

4 tablespoons icing (confectioners') sugar
2 tablespoons cocoa powder
600 ml (1 pint) double (heavy) cream

TO DECORATE:

cocoa powder, to dust
175 g (6 oz) fresh cherries
dark chocolate curls (see page 142)

EQUIPMENT | 2 x 18 cm (7 inch) round, deep cake tins

PREHEAT the oven to 170°C (335°F/Gas 3). Grease the cake tins and line the bases with baking parchment. Melt the butter over a medium heat and set aside to cool slightly. Place the sugar and eggs in a clean bowl and whisk briefly on a low speed with an electric hand mixer. Set the bowl snugly over a pan of just-boiled water. Continue whisking on a low speed for 2–3 minutes, then increase the speed for 3–4 minutes or until the mixture is pale, has increased in volume and leaves a trail when the beaters are lifted out of the bowl. Remove the bowl from the pan and continue to whisk the mixture for 2–3 minutes or until it has cooled to room temperature. Pour the melted butter down the side of the bowl and fold briefly. Then sift in the flour and cocoa powder and fold again until just incorporated (avoid over-mixing as you will lose all of the air).

Divide the mixture evenly between the prepared cake tins and bake in the oven for 25–35 minutes or until risen and springy. The cakes will have shrunk away from the sides when they are ready. Leave the cakes to cool in their tins on a wire rack.

While the cakes are cooling, make the kirsch-poached cherries. Heat the sugar and 120 ml (4 fl oz) water in a saucepan over a medium heat until the sugar has dissolved. Add the kirsch and cherries and simmer gently for 2–3 minutes or until the cherries are tender but still hold their shape.

Strain the cherries (keep the syrup for later) and set aside to cool.

Once the cakes are completely cool, use a cutlery knife to loosen the sides, turn out and split each cake in half to give you 4 layers in total (see pages 120–1). For the cream filling, add the icing sugar and cocoa powder to the cream in a bowl and whisk until the cream just holds its shape. To assemble the torte, brush some of the kirsch syrup over the first layer, spoon over a third of the cream and arrange a third of the poached cherries on top. Repeat with the second and third layers, ending with the final layer and top with a dusting of cocoa powder, a pile of fresh cherries and a few of the chocolate curls. Chill for 1–2 hours and take it out of the fridge 20 minutes before serving.

Pistachio Choux Buns

These bite-size choux buns make a cute centrepiece for an afternoon tea or dinner party dessert and aren't as much work as their croquembouche cousin. Once baked, the empty choux buns can be frozen: just pop them in the oven for five minutes once they've defrosted to crisp them up. Try these filled with sweetened whipped cream and dipped in chocolate for classic profiteroles or piped into éclair shapes.

FOR THE CHOUX BUNS:

70 g (2¼ oz/generous ½ cup) plain (all-purpose) flour
1 teaspoon caster (superfine) sugar
¼ teaspoon salt
55 g (2½ oz) unsalted butter
2 medium eggs

FOR THE PISTACHIO CREAM FILLING:

70 g (2½ oz) shelled pistachios, finely ground
2 tablespoons icing (confectioners') sugar
200 ml (7 fl oz) double (heavy) cream

FOR THE GLAZE:

250 g (9 oz) instant fondant (sugarpaste) icing
green paste or gel food colouring

TO DECORATE:

30 g (1 oz) shelled pistachios, roughly chopped
edible gold sprinkles

EQUIPMENT | piping bag fitted with
10 mm (½ inch) plain icing tip, and a 5 mm (¼ inch)
tip for filling the buns

PREHEAT the oven to 200°C (400°F/Gas 6) and line 2 baking trays with baking parchment. Sift the flour, sugar and salt into a bowl. Warm the butter with 150 ml (5 fl oz) water in a large saucepan over a very low heat until the butter has melted. Increase the heat and bring to the boil. Remove from the heat and immediately beat in the flour mixture until there are no lumps. Set aside to cool until just warm.

In a jug, beat the eggs. Gradually add the eggs to the flour mixture, beating constantly until the mixture is smooth, glossy and will drop off of a spoon after 3–4 seconds. Transfer the choux mixture to the piping bag fitted with a plain icing tip and pipe 24 small buns on to your prepared baking trays at least 2 cm (¾ inch) apart. Bake in the oven for 15–25 minutes or until risen, golden brown and crisp. Remove the buns from the oven and make a small hole in the base of each one with a skewer to release the moisture from inside. Return the buns, upside down, to the oven for another 5 minutes and cool on a wire rack.

Make the pistachio cream filling by whisking all the ingredients together in a clean bowl until the cream holds its shape. To make the glaze, mix the instant fondant icing with 3–3½ tablespoons warm water and a small amount of food colouring until just runny enough to coat the buns.

Assemble the choux buns just before serving. Fill the piping bag fitted with a 5 mm (¼ inch) tip with the pistachio cream and fill each choux bun. Coat with the fondant and top with some of the roughly chopped pistachios or a single gold sprinkle.

Fig and Almond Cake with Honey Vanilla Cream

This is a delicate and light cake that would easily work as a dessert.
Serve the cream on the side if you're on a health kick. I've baked the base in
a pie dish and turned it upside down to pretty up the sides.

FOR THE CAKE:

120 g (4 oz) unsalted butter
120 g (4 oz/generous ½ cup) caster (superfine) sugar
2 medium eggs, lightly beaten
seeds from ½ vanilla pod (see page 114)
70 g (2¼ oz/generous ½ cup) plain (all-purpose) flour
50 g (2 oz/scant ½ cup) ground almonds
1 teaspoon baking powder

FOR THE HONEY GLAZE:

15 g (½ oz) unsalted butter
1 tablespoon clear honey

FOR THE HONEY VANILLA CREAM:

200 ml (7 fl oz) double (heavy) cream
3 tablespoons clear honey
seeds from ½ vanilla pod (see page 114)

FOR THE TOPPING:

30 g (1 oz/generous ¼ cup) flaked almonds
9 fresh ripe figs, halved
1 tablespoon clear honey

EQUIPMENT | 23 cm (9 inch) fluted pie dish or 20 cm (8 inch) round cake tin

PREHEAT the oven to 170°C (335°F/Gas 3). Grease the pie dish or cake tin and line the base with baking parchment. Using a stand mixer or electric hand mixer, beat the butter and sugar in a bowl until the mixture is pale and fluffy. Add the beaten eggs to the butter mixture a little at a time, beating after each addition until they're well incorporated. Add the vanilla seeds and beat until combined.

Sift the flour, ground almonds and baking powder into a clean bowl. Add the flour mixture to the butter mixture and beat until just combined.

Spoon the mixture into the prepared pie dish or cake tin. Bake in the oven for 25 minutes, or until a skewer inserted into the centre of the cake comes out clean. Leave the oven on. Spread the flaked almonds for the topping out on to a baking tray and bake in the oven for 4–5 minutes until golden brown. Allow the cake to cool for 10 minutes in the tin, then turn it out on to a wire rack and leave to cool completely.

Meanwhile, make the honey glaze. Place the butter, honey in a saucepan and heat until melted. Brush on to the cake while it's cooling.

Just before serving make the honey vanilla cream (see pages 112–3). Place the cream, honey and vanilla seeds in a bowl and whisk until the cream just holds its shape. Pile the cream in the centre of the cake, top with the figs and toasted almonds and drizzle with honey.

Strawberry Rhubarb Fool with Rose-Scented Shortbread

The sweetened and slightly floral layers in this dessert make it a fine centrepiece to end an early summer dinner. It works especially well if you have a vintage style trifle bowl to show it off in, but any glass bowl will do. Make some rose-scented shortbread to serve on the side for added texture and to complement the rhubarb and strawberry flavours.

FOR THE RHUBARB FOOL:

500 g (1 lb 2 oz) rhubarb, washed, trimmed and cut into 2cm (3/4 inch) chunks
seeds from 1 vanilla pod (see page 114)
150 g (5 oz/2/3 cup) caster (superfine) sugar, plus extra to taste
300 g (10½ oz) fresh strawberries, hulled and cut in half
300 ml (10 fl oz) double (heavy) cream
2–3 tablespoons icing (confectioners') sugar

FOR THE ROSE-SCENTED SHORTBREAD:

110 g (3¾ oz) unsalted butter
55 g (2 oz/¼ cup) caster (superfine) sugar, plus extra to sprinkle
170 g (6 oz/scant 1½ cups) plain (all-purpose) flour, plus extra for dusting
pinch of salt
1 teaspoon rose extract

EQUIPMENT | 1 litre (2 pint) glass bowl

COMBINE the rhubarb, the seeds from half of the vanilla pod and the caster sugar in a medium saucepan and set aside for 20 minutes without heating. Gently cook the rhubarb in its juices over a low heat with a lid on for 5 minutes or until tender. Strain (keep the syrup) and set aside. Return the syrup to the saucepan over a high heat with the lid off. Simmer until reduced and thickened. Set aside to cool then combine with the cooked rhubarb. Taste the rhubarb compote and add more sugar to taste.

To make the shortbread, place all of the ingredients in a bowl and beat with a stand mixer or electric hand mixer until just combined. Bring the dough together with your hands, cover with cling film (plastic wrap) and chill for 20 minutes. Roll out the dough on a lightly floured surface to 5 mm (¼ inch) thick, cut out 5 cm (2 inch) rounds using a pastry cutter and transfer to a baking sheet lined with baking parchment (this should make 24 biscuits). Chill until firm. Preheat the oven to 170°C (335°F/Gas 3), sprinkle the biscuits with some caster sugar and bake in the oven for 8–10 minutes or until golden brown at the edges but still pale in the centre. Transfer to a wire rack to cool.

To assemble your fool, combine the cream, icing sugar and remaining vanilla seeds in a bowl and whisk until the cream holds its shape. Place half of the rhubarb compote into the bottom of a 1 litre bowl. Reserve a tablespoon of the rhubarb liquid to drizzle over the top and fold the remaining compote into the whipped cream. Spoon a layer of the whipped cream mixture on top of the rhubarb and arrange the strawberries, cut side out, on top. Cover with the remaining whipped cream mixture, drizzle with the rhubarb liquid and chill for at least 20 minutes. Serve with the shortbread on the side.

Apple, Parsnip and Rosemary Syrup Cake

Aromatic rosemary looks so beautiful as a decoration and lends its herby flavour to the sweetness of the apple and parsnip in this cake. Any leftover rosemary syrup makes for a delicious cocktail ingredient (try it with a gin and tonic).

FOR THE CAKE:

320 g (11 oz) unsalted butter, melted and cooled
320 g (11 oz/1²⁄₃ cups) soft light brown sugar
4 medium eggs
320 g (11 oz/generous 2½ cups) plain (all-purpose) flour
2 teaspoons bicarbonate of soda (baking soda)
1 teaspoon ground cinnamon
pinch of salt
100 g (3½ oz) peeled and coarsely grated parsnip
200 g (7 oz) peeled and coarsely grated eating apple
1 tablespoon finely chopped fresh rosemary

FOR THE ROSEMARY SYRUP:

125 g (4½ oz/generous ½ cup) caster (superfine) sugar
2 sprigs of rosemary

FOR THE CINNAMON BUTTERCREAM:

125 g (4½ oz) unsalted butter
200 g (7 oz/generous 1½ cups) icing (confectioners') sugar
2 teaspoons ground cinnamon
50 ml (2 fl oz) double (heavy) cream

TO DECORATE:

a few sprigs of crystallised rosemary (see page 146)

EQUIPMENT | 2 x 15 cm (6 inch) round, deep cake tins | cake board or stand

PREHEAT the oven to 170°C (335°F/Gas 3). Grease the cake tins and line the bases with baking parchment. Using a stand mixer or electric hand mixer, beat the butter, sugar and eggs for 2–3 minutes or until the mixture is pale and well combined. Sift the flour, bicarbonate of soda, cinnamon and salt into a clean bowl. Add the flour mixture to the butter mixture and beat to combine. Finally, fold in the parsnip, apple and rosemary. Divide the mixture evenly between the prepared cake tins. Bake in the oven for 40–50 minutes, or until a skewer inserted into the centre of each cake comes out clean. Allow the cakes to cool for 10 minutes in their tins, then turn them out on to a wire rack and leave to cool completely.

To make the syrup, place the sugar, 250 ml (9 fl oz) cold water and rosemary in a saucepan and simmer gently, stirring occasionally, until the sugar has dissolved. Set aside to cool then discard the rosemary sprigs.

To make the buttercream, using a stand mixer or electric hand mixer, beat the butter for 3–4 minutes until pale and creamy. Add the remaining ingredients and continue to beat for another 2–3 minutes until smooth.

Level the cakes by cutting off the domed tops and split each cake in half so that you have 4 layers in total (see pages 120–1). Fix the bottom layer to the cake board or stand, brush the cut side with the rosemary syrup and spread with one quarter of the buttercream. Add the second layer and repeat, then continue with the third and fourth layers, finishing with a thin layer of buttercream. Use an offset spatula to smooth the excess buttercream around the sides of the cake, leaving the cake layers visible. Decorate with crystallised rosemary.

Red Velvet and Raspberry Layer Cake

———|———

I love the rich and slightly sour flavour that buttermilk brings to this red velvet cake. If you can't find buttermilk, just add two teaspoons of white wine vinegar or lemon juice to 180 ml (6 fl oz) of whole milk, stir and leave to stand for 5 minutes and you'll have a handy substitute. The sweetness of the cream cheese buttercream is the perfect match for tart raspberries.

FOR THE CAKE:

———

85 g (3 oz) unsalted butter
225 g (8 oz/1 cup) caster (superfine) sugar
2 medium eggs, lightly beaten
225 g (8 oz/scant 2 cups) plain
(all-purpose) flour
1 teaspoon bicarbonate of soda (baking soda)
1 teaspoon salt
2 tablespoons cocoa powder
180 ml (6 fl oz) buttermilk
1 1/2 tablespoons red food colouring
1 teaspoon vanilla extract

FOR THE VANILLA CREAM-CHEESE
BUTTERCREAM:

———

125 g (4 1/2 oz) unsalted butter
200 g (7 oz/generous 1 1/2 cups) icing
(confectioners') sugar
1/2 teaspoon vanilla extract
75 g (2 1/2 oz) full-fat cream cheese, chilled

TO FILL AND DECORATE:

———

250 g (9 oz) fresh raspberries
icing (confectioners') sugar, to dust

EQUIPMENT | 2 x 15 cm (6 inch) round, deep cake tins |
cake board or stand | piping bag fitted
with an 18 mm (3/4 inch) large star tip

PREHEAT the oven to 170°C (335°F/Gas 3). Grease the cake tins and line the bases with baking parchment. Using a stand mixer or electric hand mixer, beat the butter and sugar until the mixture is pale and creamy. Add the beaten eggs to the butter mixture a little at a time, beating after each addition until they're well incorporated.

Sift the flour, bicarbonate of soda, salt and cocoa powder into a clean bowl. In a jug combine the butter-milk, food colouring and vanilla extract. Add the flour and buttermilk mixtures to the butter mixture, half at a time. Beat until just combined, scraping down the sides of the bowl as you go.

Divide the mixture evenly between the prepared cake tins and bake for 30 minutes, or until a skewer inserted into the centre of each cake comes out clean. Allow the cakes to cool for 10 minutes in their tins, then turn them out on to a wire rack and leave to cool completely. To make the vanilla cream-cheese buttercream, beat the butter for 3–4 minutes until pale and creamy. Add the icing sugar and vanilla extract and beat for 2–3 minutes until smooth. Then add the cream cheese and beat until just combined.

Level the cakes by cutting off the domed tops (see pages 120–1). Fix one cake to the cake board or stand with a small amount of buttercream. Spread with half of the buttercream and top with raspberries. Place the second cake on top and press down gently. Fill a piping bag with the remaining buttercream and pipe 8 evenly spaced peaks (see pages 134–7). Decorate with the remaining raspberries and dust with icing sugar.

Coconut Cake with Scalloped Piping

This is the perfect match of a simple and tasty cake with impressively fancy icing.
Practise piping the dots on baking parchment first (see pages 136–7) – it's much easier to achieve
the scalloped piping than it looks.

FOR THE CAKE:

175 g (6 oz) unsalted butter
375 g (13 oz/1⅔ cups) caster (superfine) sugar
4 medium eggs, lightly beaten
375 g (13 oz/3 cups) plain (all-purpose) flour
4 teaspoons baking powder
½ teaspoon salt
250 ml (9 fl oz) buttermilk
1 teaspoon vanilla extract
120 g (4½ oz/1¼ cups) desiccated coconut

FOR THE VANILLA BUTTERCREAM FILLING:

175 g (6 oz) unsalted butter
250 g (9 oz/generous 2 cups) icing (confectioners') sugar
100 ml (3½ fl oz) double (heavy) cream
1 teaspoon vanilla extract

FOR THE SWISS MERINGUE BUTTERCREAM:

400 g (14 oz) unsalted butter
10 medium egg whites
450 g (1 lb/scant 2 cups) caster (superfine) sugar
2 teaspoons vanilla extract

EQUIPMENT | 2 x 18 cm (7 inch) round, deep cake tins | piping bag fitted with
a plain 10 mm (½ inch) icing tip | cake board or stand

PREHEAT the oven to 170°C (335°F/Gas 3). Grease the cake tins and line the bases with baking parchment. Using a stand mixer or an electric hand mixer, beat the butter and sugar until pale and fluffy. Add the eggs to the butter mixture a little at a time, beating after each addition until they are well incorporated.

Sift the flour, baking powder and salt into a clean bowl. Add half the flour mixture to the sugar and butter mixture and beat. Add the buttermilk and vanilla extract, continuing to beat, and then add the remaining flour mixture and beat until just incorporated. Finally, fold in the desiccated coconut.

Divide the mixture evenly between the prepared cake tins. Bake in the oven for 45–50 minutes, or until a skewer inserted into the centre of each cake comes out clean. Allow the cakes to cool for 10 minutes in their tins, then turn them out onto a wire rack and leave to cool completely.

While the cakes are cooling, make the vanilla buttercream filling and the Swiss meringue buttercream. To make the vanilla buttercream filling, using a stand mixer or electric hand mixer, beat the butter for 3–4 minutes until pale and creamy. Add the remaining ingredients and continue to beat for another 2–3 minutes until smooth.

To make the Swiss meringue buttercream, using a stand mixer or electric hand mixer beat the butter for 4–5 minutes until pale and fluffy. Place the egg whites and sugar in a clean heatproof bowl over a saucepan of simmering water, ensuring that the water does not touch the bottom of the bowl. Whisk and gently heat the mixture until the sugar has dissolved into the egg white (you can check this by feeling some of the egg white between your fingers – it shouldn't feel grainy).

Remove the bowl from the heat and using a stand mixer with the whisk attachment or an electric hand whisk, start beating on a low speed for 1–2 minutes, then increase the speed until the bowl has cooled down to room temperature and the mixture forms stiff peaks (about 10 minutes in total). Add the butter a tablespoon at a time ensuring that each addition is well incorporated before adding the next one. It might look like the buttercream has curdled at this point but keep whisking and it will come back together. Once smooth, beat in the vanilla extract.

Level the cakes with a cake leveller or a serrated knife and split each cake in half so that you have 4 layers (see pages 120–1). Fix your cake to a cake board or cake stand with a small amount of buttercream. Spread a generous amount of the vanilla buttercream between the cake layers, then cover the outside with a thin layer. Chill for 20–30 minutes or until firm. Meanwhile, fill the piping bag with the Swiss meringue buttercream (see pages 134–5) and cover the cake with a scalloped effect (see page 139).

Chocolate Beetroot Cake

├────────────┤

This cake uses beetroot, which brings an earthy flavour and hint of that
bright beetroot pink to the layers when you cut a slice.

FOR THE CAKE:

400 g (14 oz) unsalted butter, melted and cooled
400 g (14 oz/scant 2 cups) soft light brown sugar
5 medium eggs, lightly beaten
1 teaspoon vanilla extract
350 g (12 oz/scant 3 cups) plain (all-purpose) flour
50 g (2 oz/scant ½ cup) cocoa powder
2½ teaspoons bicarbonate of soda (baking powder)
1 teaspoon salt
300 g (10½ oz) raw or cooked beetroot, peeled and coarsely grated
(about 3–4 medium beetroots)

FOR THE RICH CHOCOLATE BUTTERCREAM:

250 g (9 oz) dark chocolate, finely chopped
250 g (9 oz) unsalted butter
250 g (9 oz/generous cup) golden icing (confectioners') sugar

TO DECORATE:

pink or red fresh flowers, pesticide free (see page 150)

EQUIPMENT | 2 x 18 cm (7 inch) round, deep cake tins | cake stand or board

PREHEAT the oven to 170°C (335°F/Gas 3). Grease the cake tins and line the bases with baking parchment. Using a stand mixer or electric hand mixer, beat the butter, sugar, eggs and vanilla extract for 2–3 minutes or until the mixture is pale and well combined. Sift the flour, cocoa powder, bicarbonate of soda and salt into a clean bowl. Add the flour mixture to the sugar mixture and beat to combine. Fold in the beetroot, scraping down the sides of the bowl as you go.

Divide the mixture evenly between the prepared tins. Bake in the oven for 50–60 minutes, or until a skewer inserted into the centre of each cake comes out clean. Allow the cakes to cool for 10 minutes in their tins, then turn them out on to a wire rack and leave to cool completely.

While the cakes are baking and cooling, make the rich chocolate buttercream. Place the chocolate in a heatproof bowl over a saucepan of simmering water, making sure that the water does not touch the bottom of the bowl. Stir the chocolate until it is almost melted, then remove the pan from the heat. Remove the bowl from the saucepan to ensure that the chocolate doesn't become overheated, and continue to stir until the chocolate is completely melted. Set aside to cool. Using a stand mixer or electric hand mixer, beat the butter in a bowl for 3–4 minutes until pale and creamy. Add the golden icing sugar and melted chocolate and continue to beat for another 2–3 minutes until smooth.

Level the cakes by cutting off the domed tops (see pages 120–1). Fix your first cake layer to a cake board or cake stand with a small amount of buttercream. Spread the first layer with a generous amount of the buttercream and place the second layer on top. Cover the cake with a thin layer of buttercream and chill for 30 minutes or until firm. Cover the cake with the remaining buttercream (see pages 130–3) and decorate with the fresh flowers.

Blueberry Cinnamon Swirl Cake

├────────┤

This cake uses the naturally vibrant colour of blueberries to add a surprise swirl on the inside as well as the buttercream swirls on the outside. I was inspired by *Charlie and the Chocolate Factory's* Violet character to add the cute balloons, which are actually water-bombs.

FOR THE BLUEBERRY PURÉE:

175 g (6 oz) fresh blueberries
1 teaspoon ground cinnamon
2 tablespoons caster (superfine) sugar

FOR THE CAKE:

250 g (9 oz) unsalted butter
450 g (1 lb/scant 2 cups) caster (superfine) sugar
4 medium eggs, lightly beaten
375 g (13 oz/ 3 cups) plain (all-purpose) flour
2 teaspoons baking powder
pinch of salt
180 ml (6½ fl oz) whole milk
1 teaspoon vanilla extract

FOR THE VANILLA BUTTERCREAM:

300 g (10½ oz) unsalted butter
480 g (1 lb 1 oz/scant 4 cups) icing (confectioners') sugar
120 ml (4 fl oz) double (heavy) cream
1 teaspoon vanilla extract

TO DECORATE:

skewers
water-bomb sized balloons
fresh blueberries (optional)

EQUIPMENT | *2 x 18 cm (7 inch) round cake tins*

PREHEAT the oven to 170°C (335°F/Gas 3). Grease the cake tins and line the bases with baking parchment. Make the blueberry purée by combining the blueberries, cinnamon, caster sugar and 1 tablespoon of water in a saucepan. Heat gently until the blueberries are soft. Crush the blueberries with the back of a fork and set aside to cool.

Using a stand mixer or electric hand mixer, beat the butter and sugar for 3–4 minutes until the mixture is pale and fluffy. Add the eggs to the butter mixture a little at a time, beating after each addition until they're well incorporated.

Sift the flour, baking powder and salt into a clean bowl. Add half of the flour mixture to the butter mixture. Add 120 ml (4 fl oz) of the milk, the vanilla extract and the remaining flour and beat until just combined. Spoon a third of the cake mixture into a clean bowl and beat in the cooled blueberry purée. Add the remaining milk to the vanilla cake mixture and beat until just combined.

To create the swirl effect, divide the vanilla mixture evenly between the prepared cake tins and top each tin with the blueberry mixture. Gently fold the 2 layers together. Bake in the oven for 50 minutes, or until a skewer inserted into the centre of each cake comes out clean. Allow the cakes to cool for 10 minutes in their tins, then turn them out on to a wire rack and leave to cool completely.

While the cakes are cooling, make the vanilla buttercream. Using a stand mixer or electric hand mixer, beat the butter for 3–4 minutes until pale and creamy. Add the remaining ingredients and continue to beat for another 2–3 minutes until smooth.

Level the cakes by cutting off the domed tops with a cake leveller or a serrated knife (see pages 120–1). Spread the bottom layer of the cake generously with buttercream. Top with the second cake. Cover the cake whole with a thin layer of buttercream and chill for 30 minutes or until firm. Once firm, spread the cake with the remaining buttercream (see pages 130-3) and use a palette knife to create a swirled effect (see page 138). Decorate with the mini balloons attached to skewers or a scattering of extra blueberries.

White Rose Cake

——┤├——

I love this dip-dye look. Inside is a rose flavoured cake that uses mostly
egg white, giving the sponge a pale shade which lends itself well to being coloured.
See page 116 for tips on how to turn this into a rainbow cake.

FOR THE CAKE:
———

125 g (4 1/2 oz) unsalted butter
250 g (9 oz/generous cup) caster (superfine) sugar
1 medium egg and 3 medium egg whites, lightly beaten
225 g (8 oz/scant 2 cups) plain (all-purpose) flour
2 1/2 teaspoons baking powder
1/2 teaspoon salt
180 ml (6 fl oz) whole milk
1 teaspoon rose extract

FOR THE ROSE BUTTERCREAM:
———

375 g (13 oz) unsalted butter
600 g (1 lb 3 oz/scant 5 cups) icing (confectioners') sugar
150 ml (5 fl oz) double (heavy) cream
2–3 teaspoons rose extract
pink paste or gel food colouring

TO DECORATE:
———

pink and white crystallised rose petals (see page 151)

EQUIPMENT | 2 x 13 cm (5 inch) round, deep cake tins |
cake board or stand

PREHEAT the oven to 170°C (335°F/Gas 3). Grease the cake tins and line with baking parchment. Using a stand mixer or electric hand mixer, beat the butter and sugar in a bowl until pale and fluffy. Add the eggs to the mixture a little at a time, until they're well incorporated.

Sift the flour, baking powder and salt into bowl. Add half of the flour mixture to the butter mixture and beat until just combined. Add half of the milk and the rose extract, continuing to beat, and then add the remaining flour and milk.

Divide the mixture evenly between the prepared cake tins. Bake in the oven for 45–50 minutes, or until a skewer inserted into the centre of each cake comes out clean. Allow the cakes to cool for 10 minutes in their tins, then turn them out on to a wire rack and leave to cool completely.

While the cakes are cooling, make the rose buttercream. Using a stand mixer or electric hand mixer, beat the butter for 3–4 minutes until pale and creamy. Add the icing sugar and cream and continue to beat for another 2–3 minutes until smooth. Add the rose extract gradually to taste.

Level the cakes by cutting off the domed tops and split each layer in half so that you have 4 layers in total (see pages 120–1). Fix the bottom layer to the cake board or stand with a small amount of buttercream and spread with a generous amount of the buttercream. Add the second layer and repeat, and repeat again with the third layer, finishing with the final cake layer. Cover the cake with a thin layer of buttercream (see pages 130–3) and chill for 30 minutes or until firm.

Split the remaining buttercream into 3 bowls, leaving half of the buttercream white and colouring a quarter deep pink and a quarter pale pink (see page 116). Spread the white buttercream over the top and halfway down the sides of the cake. With a clean spatula, spread the deep pink buttercream around the bottom quarter of the cake. Spread the pale pink buttercream between the white and deep pink colours, clean your spatula and smooth the cake, removing excess buttercream as you go. Decorate with the crystallised rose petals.

Chestnut and Pear Cheesecake

———|———

The poached pears in this autumnal cheesecake look so inviting poking up through the layers of chocolate and chestnut. The chocolate glaze is worth trying on other cakes, too. Chill the cake before pouring over the glaze to freeze-frame the chocolaty drips.

FOR THE POACHED PEARS:
———

7 small, firm pears
500 g (1 lb 2 oz/scant ¼ cup) caster (superfine) sugar

FOR THE BASE:
———

180 g (6½ oz) digestive biscuits
90 g (3¼ oz) unsalted butter
2 tablespoons cocoa powder

FOR THE FILLING:
———

100 g (3½ oz) dark chocolate, finely chopped
250 g (9 oz/1 cup) cream cheese
150 g (5 oz/generous ¾ cup) soft light brown sugar
450 ml (15½ fl oz) double (heavy) cream
150 g (5 oz) chestnut spread

FOR THE CHOCOLATE GLAZE:
———

100 g (3½ oz) dark chocolate, finely chopped
50 g (2 oz) unsalted butter

EQUIPMENT | 20 cm (8 inch) round, deep cake tin

TO poach the pears, peel, leaving the stalks intact, then slice off the bottoms and hollow out to remove the core and seeds. Pour the sugar and 1 litre (34 fl oz) cold water into a large saucepan and heat gently to dissolve the sugar, stirring occasionally. Add the pears to the saucepan and place some baking parchment onto the surface of the syrup and a lid on the pan. Simmer for 15 minutes, or until the pears are tender. Leave the pears in the syrup and set aside to cool.

To make the base, line the cake tin with cling film (plastic wrap). Place the digestive biscuits in a plastic bag and crush into crumbs with a rolling pin or the back of a wooden spoon. Melt the butter in a large saucepan and stir in the crushed biscuits and cocoa powder. Press the biscuit mixture into the bottom of the prepared cake tin, making the base slightly higher at the sides. Chill for 20 minutes or until firm.

Meanwhile, make the filling. Melt the chocolate by placing it in a heatproof bowl over a saucepan of simmering water, making sure that the water does not touch the bottom of the bowl (see page 115). Stir the chocolate until it is almost melted, then remove the pan from the heat. Remove the bowl from the saucepan to ensure that the chocolate doesn't become overheated, and continue to stir until the chocolate is completely melted then set aside to cool.

Place the cream cheese and sugar in a bowl and beat by hand to combine. In a clean bowl, whisk the double cream until it forms soft peaks and fold into the cream cheese mixture. Split the cream cheese mixture into 2 bowls and fold the melted and cooled chocolate into one half, and the chestnut spread into the other half.

To assemble, spread the chocolate filling over the chilled base. Plunge the poached pears into the chocolate filling and chill for 20 minutes or until firm. Spread the chestnut filling over the top of the chocolate filling and chill again for at least 2 hours or overnight.

Just before serving, make the chocolate glaze. Melt the chocolate and butter in a heatproof bowl over a saucepan of simmering water as before. Set aside to cool slightly. Remove the cheesecake from the cake tin and set on a serving plate or cake stand. Pour over the chocolate glaze and serve.

Citrus Confetti Cake

———

Confetti sprinkles are an easy way to give cakes a fun party look. I like to match the colour of my sprinkles to the flavours of the cake inside to give people a preview of what they're about to taste, so here we have pastel citrus colours. The meringue-based buttercream is beautiful for piping and leaves you with some leftover egg yolks to make your own curd.

FOR THE CAKE:

450 g (1 lb) unsalted butter
620 g (1 lb 6 oz/2¾ cups) caster (superfine) sugar
8 medium eggs, lightly beaten
620 g (1 lb 6 oz/5 cups) plain (all-purpose) flour
5 teaspoons baking powder
1 teaspoon salt
250 ml (9 fl oz) whole milk
grated zest of 4 unwaxed oranges
grated zest of 4 unwaxed lemons

FOR THE MERINGUE BUTTERCREAM:

400 g (14 oz) unsalted butter
10 medium egg whites
450 g (1 lb/scant 2 cups) caster (superfine) sugar
2 teaspoons vanilla extract

FOR THE PINK GRAPEFRUIT CURD:

5 medium egg yolks
170 g (6 oz/¾ cup) caster (superfine) sugar
grated zest and juice of 1 pink grapefruit
1 tablespoon lemon juice
110 g (3½ oz) unsalted butter, cubed

TO DECORATE:

fondant confetti in pastel citrus shades of yellows,
oranges and pinks (see pages 144–145)

EQUIPMENT | 2 x 20 cm (8 inch) round, deep cake tins
cake board or stand | piping bag fitted with 1 cm (½ inch) plain tip

PREHEAT the oven to 170°C (335°F/Gas 3). Grease the cake tins and line the bases with baking parchment. Using a stand mixer or electric hand mixer, beat the butter and sugar for 3–4 minutes or until the mixture is pale and fluffy. Add the eggs a little at a time, beating after each addition until they're well incorporated.

Sift the flour, baking powder and salt into a clean bowl. Add half of the flour mixture to the butter mixture and beat until just combined. Add the milk, continuing to beat, and then add the remaining flour mixture and the orange and lemon zest. Scrape down the sides of the bowl as you go and beat until just combined.

Divide the mixture evenly between the prepared cake tins. Bake in the oven for 70–75 minutes, or until a skewer inserted into the centre of each cake comes out clean. Allow the cakes to cool for 10 minutes in their tins, then turn them out onto a wire rack and leave to cool completely.

While the cakes are baking and cooling, make the meringue buttercream and pink grapefruit curd. To make the meringue buttercream, using a stand mixer or electric hand mixer, beat the butter for 4–5 minutes until pale and fluffy. Place the egg whites and sugar in a clean heatproof bowl over a saucepan of simmering water, making sure that the water does not touch the bottom of the bowl. Whisk and gently heat the mixture until the sugar has dissolved into the egg white (you can check this by feeling some of the egg white between your fingers – it shouldn't feel grainy). Remove the bowl from the heat and, using a stand mixer or electric hand mixer, start whisking on a low speed for 1–2 minutes, then increase the speed until the bowl has cooled down to room temperature and the mixture forms stiff peaks (about 10 minutes in total). Add the butter 1 tablespoon at a time ensuring that each addition is well incorporated before adding the next one. It might look like the buttercream has curdled at this point but keep whisking and it will come back together. Once the buttercream is smooth and all of the butter has been incorporated, beat in the vanilla extract.

To make the pink grapefruit curd, place the egg yolks, sugar, zest and juices into a heatproof bowl over a saucepan of simmering water (make sure that the water isn't touching the bottom of the bowl). Stir constantly and add the butter a cube at a time, heating gently until all of the butter has been incorporated and the mixture has thickened (about 10 minutes). Strain into a shallow container and cover with cling film (plastic wrap) to prevent a skin from forming and set aside to cool. Chill until needed.

Level the cakes by cutting off the domed tops (see pages 120–1) and split each cake in half so that you have 4 layers in total. Fix your first cake layer to a cake board or cake stand with a small amount of buttercream. Fill a piping bag with the meringue buttercream (see pages 134–5) and pipe a line around the edge of the first cake layer (this will stop your curd filling from escaping). Fill with 2–3 tablespoons of the pink grapefruit curd. Gently press the second layer on top of the first and repeat, then repeat again with the third layer, finishing with the final cake layer (see pages 122–3). Cover the cake with a thin layer of the meringue buttercream and chill for 30 minutes or until firm. Finally, cover the cake with a thicker layer of meringue buttercream with a smooth finish and use a plain icing tip to pipe a border around the top and bottom edge of the cake. Decorate with the confetti sprinkles.

2

Flavour & Colour

———— ⊢———⊣ ————

A cake can be completely transformed by swapping out flavours, adding colour to buttercream or even the cake layers themselves. Here are a few techniques for adding flavour and colour from flavouring and whipping cream to using food colouring to achieve subtle or vibrant shades.

HOW TO FLAVOUR AND WHIP CREAM

Flavoured and whipped cream makes for an indulgent topping or accompaniment to cakes. It's an easy way to make a cake into a dessert or to bring in an extra flavour. You'll need about 300 ml (10 fl oz) to cover the top of a 20 cm (8 inch) cake. Around 150 ml (5 fl oz) is enough to cover a 15 cm (6 inch) cake or to serve in a dish on the side.

For 300 ml (10 fl oz) double (heavy) cream you will need about 1 tablespoon of icing (confectioners') sugar. It's important to sweeten cream to serve with a cake or dessert, otherwise the contrast can make the cream taste savoury. Sweetening the cream will also bring out the other flavours.

There are so many different flavours that you can experiment with. Try any of the following:

• Vanilla seeds
• Extracts like rose, orange blossom and almond
• The grated zest of a lemon, lime or orange
• A few tablespoons of lemon curd, caramel sauce or runny honey (you may need to warm the caramel slightly and let it cool to room temperature so that it will combine easily with the cream)
• A tablespoon of cocoa powder
• A teaspoon of ground cinnamon or ground cardamom seeds
• A teaspoon or two of elderflower or rhubarb cordial
• A teaspoon or two of espresso (it pairs nicely with chocolate cake)
• A teaspoon or two of kirsch, Grand Marnier or amaretto for a boozy kick
• Sprinkle strawberries, raspberries or blackberries with some caster (superfine) sugar and fold them into already-sweetened and whipped cream for a fruity rippled effect

STEPS 1 AND 2: Add the flavouring and icing sugar and to the cream, have a taste and make any adjustments before you start whisking. It's much easier to adjust the flavour and sweetness at this stage.

STEPS 3 AND 4: Whisk until the cream forms soft peaks and just starts to hold its shape. Make sure you lift your whisk above the cream to get plenty of air in there. It's very easy to over-whisk and end up with a fluffy-looking split texture so I prefer to whisk by hand so that I can keep an eye on things. Don't worry if you end up over-whipping, just add a little extra cream to bring it back to the right consistency. Transfer the whipped cream to your cake or serving dish and serve straight away.

HOW TO SPLIT A VANILLA POD

Vanilla pods (or beans) are one of my favourite smells and I love it when you can see flecks of the dark seeds in a cake or dessert. You can use the seeds to flavour whipped cream (see page 112), buttercream, curds and cake batters or even use the empty pod for punchy flavouring once the seeds have been removed.

1. To deseed a vanilla pod, score down the length with a sharp knife then scrape the seeds from the inside by running your knife along the surface.

2. Collect the scraped seeds on the end of your knife and use to flavour creams and batters. Keep the empty vanilla pods to flavour sugar by placing them together in a sealed jar. Or leave it to dry out and grind up into a powder to add to your baking.

HOW TO MELT CHOCOLATE

For baking, I like to use dark chocolate with a minimum of 70 per cent cocoa solids. Chocolate brands vary in flavour quite a lot so try a few until you find one that you like and keep a stash in your store cupboard. Chocolate needs to be heated gently as it can become overheated and grainy quite easily.

1. Using a sharp, serrated knife, chop your chocolate very finely. I find it easiest to do this while it's still in a block rather than breaking the block up into squares first. Finely chopped chocolate will melt quickly and evenly so you're less likely to overheat it.

2. Place your chocolate in a heatproof bowl over a pan of just simmering water. Make sure that the water doesn't touch the bottom of the bowl. Gently stir the chocolate and remove from the heat when about two thirds of it has melted to avoid overheating. Continue to stir until all the chocolate has melted.

HOW TO USE FOOD COLOURING

I find that the best way to colour buttercream is to use paste (sometimes called gel) food colourings. This is what the professionals use and it's really concentrated so you can achieve an intense deep colour as well as beautifully subtle pastel shades without having to add lots of liquid to your buttercream. They cost a bit morethan liquid colours but last for a long time. Avoid the temptation of buying lots of different colours and start with a few basics, which you can mix to get the colour you want.

Keep in mind that butter actually has a yellow tint to it so adding a tiny bit of blue will actually make your buttercream a nice minty green. Cocktail sticks are handy for adding colourings to your buttercream as you can throw them away as soon as you have dipped them into the pot once. A little goes a long way, so start off with a small amount and build up the shade that you want gradually.

Paste colours aren't just for buttercream. For a colourful surprise, make a cake with plain white buttercream on the outside and colour the cake layers on the inside. The White Rose Cake on page 98 can easily be adapted into a rainbow cake. Swap the rose extract for vanilla and, once you have made your cake batter, weigh it into 6 separate bowls and use a generous amount of paste to colour each batch red, orange, yellow, green, red and violet. Working in batches, bake each colour batter in a separate tin and reduce the baking time to 15-20 minutes.

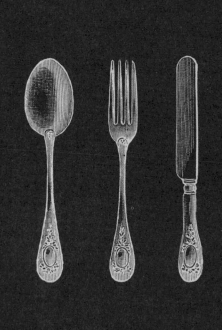

3

Constructing & Levelling Cakes

These basic techniques will make such a difference to the
final look of your cakes. This chapter has lots of tips and
step-by-step photos from how to level and split cakes evenly
to building impressive tiered cakes.

HOW TO LEVEL &
SPLIT A CAKE

I love that moment when you cut into a cake to take out the first slice and see that all of your hard work has paid off – even stripes created by layers of tender sponge and rich buttercream. Baked cakes will inevitably have a slight dome to them (if they are very domed it's a sign that your oven might be too hot), so it's a good idea to level your cake before you start to decorate. If you can, bake your cake the day before decorating, let it cool completely, wrap it in cling film (plastic wrap) and level and split it the following day when it will be less fragile to handle.

YOU WILL NEED: 2 X CAKES | CAKE LEVELLER OR SERRATED KNIFE

1. Start by levelling off the domed tops. Adjust the height of your cake leveller so that it will slice off the domed top while keeping as much of the cake as possible.

2. Cut 1–2 cm (1/2–3/4 inch) into the crust of the cake with a sawing motion. Make sure that the cake leveller stays upright with the feet on the work surface. Cakes can be quite fragile and cutting through the crust first will stop your cake from crumbling too much.

3. Turn the cake to cut through the crust all the way around before you cut through the middle.

4. Remove the domed top and repeat with your cake leveller at the same height for the second cake.

5. Next, adjust your cake leveller to split your levelled cakes in half cutting through the crust first as above.

6. Now you have 4 level cake layers of equal height, ready to fill and cover. Place the bottom of one cake, crust side down, onto the bottom of your stack and the bottom of the other cake, crust side up, on the top so that you have a nice smooth surface to work with. If you're baking your cake in advance, now is a good time to wrap the whole thing in 2 layers of cling film (plastic wrap), freeze for up to 3 months or store in an airtight container for up to 3 days.

TIP: If you don't have a cake leveller, hold a serrated knife against the side of the cake and turn the cake on your work surface to cut through the crust. This will make sure that your initial cut stays at the same height all of the way round. Then cut all the way through, keeping one hand on top of the cake for support.

HOW TO FILL CAKES WITH JAMS OR CURDS

Sometimes it's nice to see a bit of jam or curd oozing generously out of the sides of layer cakes, but if you're covering the sides of your cake in buttercream or ganache it's a good idea to add a 'dam' to stop the runnier filling from leaking out.

1. Fill a piping bag fitted with a large plain icing tip with buttercream or ganache (see pages 134–5), and pipe a line around the outside of the cake layer.

2. Fill the layer with a thin layer of your jam or curd.

3. Spread out the jam or curd to meet the piped line with the back of a spoon.

4. Place the next layer on top and press down gently to make sure that the filling is sealed in all the way round. Repeat these steps for the remaining layers.

HOW TO ASSEMBLE
TIERED CAKES

Cakes can be pretty heavy, and tall cakes with lots of layers and tiers need a bit of extra support to stay upright and level. This technique works for tiered cakes which start with a larger cake on the bottom and end with a smaller cake on the top, but is also great for super-tall multi-layer cakes where all of the layers are the same width. Start with your cake tiers levelled and split (see pages 120–1), filled (see pages 122–3) and either left 'naked' like the Stacked Victoria Sandwich (see page 51) or covered with buttercream or ganache (see pages 130–3). Each tier should be attached to a thin cake board, the same size as the cake layers, with a small amount of buttercream or ganache.

YOU WILL NEED: CAKE TIERS | THIN CAKE BOARDS | PLASTIC LOLLYPOP STICKS OR CAKE DOWELS (4 PER TIER APART FROM THE TOP ONE) | A BIT OF EXTRA BUTTERCREAM OR GANACHE

1. Starting with the bottom tier, insert a lollypop stick or cake dowel just inside the edge of where the second tier will sit. It should go all the way through the cake until it reaches the board. Mark the stick with a sharp knife at the surface of the cake and take it out again.

2. Cut the first stick where you made the mark with the knife and trim the other 3 sticks to be exactly the same length.

3. Push all 4 sticks, evenly spaced, into the bottom tier. This will support the second tier.

4. At this point, you can spread a small amount of buttercream between the tiers to help keep everything in its place. If you need to transport the cake, it's best to assemble the tiers and do the final decoration when you get the cake to its destination.

5. Place the second tier on top of the first tier and repeat the process of inserting the lollypop sticks or dowels with the second tier, inserting 4 more trimmed sticks to support the top tier.

6. Dust with icing sugar and decorate with fresh flowers and fruit. You can use hidden cocktail sticks to hold everything in place.

TIP: It's easier to assemble your cake tiers if they have been chilled for 30 minutes first.

CHAPTER

4

Decorating with Buttercream

| |

This chapter covers the all-important skill of how to fill a
piping bag with buttercream, plus piping techniques from
scallops to swirls that will make any cake look amazing.

HOW TO MAKE BUTTERCREAM

Getting your buttercream to the perfect consistency will make it much easier to use as a filling in between cake layers, to cover your cake with a palette knife for a smooth look and for piping designs that hold their shape beautifully. It also means that your cake will have a nicer flavour and texture so that it tastes as good as it looks. Most of the buttercream recipes in this book are based on a combination of unsalted butter, icing (confectioners') sugar and double (heavy) cream. As butter and cream are the main flavours here it's worth looking out for good quality brands. Start with butter that is soft but still cool enough to hold its shape.

1. Using a stand mixer or electric hand mixer to beat your ingredients together for a minimum of 5 minutes will incorporate air into the mixture, giving your buttercream a pale colour and lighter texture. If you find that your buttercream is too thin, it may be that it contains too much liquid. Try adding some more softened butter and sugar. If it's too soft, it may have got too warm. Try covering and chilling it for 15 minutes before beating again. If the consistency is quite dense, the butter might be too cold or it might not have been beaten for long enough. Try leaving your buttercream covered at room temperature for 30 minutes before beating again.

2. Just before you're ready to use your buttercream, beat it on a low speed for 2–3 minutes to reduce large bubbles and make the texture smoother.

3. Buttercream is best used as soon as you've made it but it will keep covered and chilled for a few days or can be frozen for up to a month. When you're ready to use it, leave it to come up to room temperature and beat it again.

HOW TO FILL AND COVER
A CAKE WITH BUTTERCREAM
OR CHOCOLATE GANACHE

Start with smooth, cool, room-temperature buttercream. If you're working with a particularly fragile cake, chill the cake layers first, wrapped in cling film (plastic wrap), to make them a bit more sturdy. If you're not putting the cake directly on to a cake plate or stand, using a thin cake board makes it easier to move the filled and covered cake around. Attach the first layer, bottom side down, to the board, plate or stand with a small amount of buttercream.

STEPS 1 – 6

YOU WILL NEED: ANGLED PALETTE KNIVES IN 2 SIZES | AN ICE CREAM SCOOP | A RUBBER SPATULA | A SMALL BOWL | A CAKE BOARD (SAME SIZE AS YOUR CAKE) BAKING PARCHMENT OR A CAKE TURNTABLE

1. Brush away any crumbs from the surface of the cake layer. Use an ice cream scoop or large spoon to portion out your buttercream for the first layer. I find that 3 scoops work well for an 18 cm (7 inch) cake.

2. Pile the buttercream up in the centre of the layer and spread it to the edges using smooth paddling motions with your small offset palette knife.

3. Gently press the second cake layer on to the buttercream.

4. Portion out the second layer of buttercream using the same number of scoops.

5. Spread the buttercream to the edges of the cake as before.

6. Continue to build up the layers, finishing with the bottom of the second cake facing upwards. If you are making a 'naked' cake without buttercream on the sides you can stop here, tidy up the buttercream with a clean palette knife and add a final layer of buttercream, or dusting of cocoa powder or icing (confectioners') sugar, on top.

continued overleaf

7. Spread a very thin layer of buttercream over the whole cake. This is called a 'crumb coat' and helps to seal in the crumbs so that your final coating is beautifully smooth and crumb free.

8. Scrape any excess buttercream into a separate bowl so that you don't mix any crumbs in with your clean batch. Once you have scraped off the excess buttercream and wiped the cake board, stand or plate clean, chill the cake for 30 minutes or until firm.

9. Now that your cake is chilled, with all of the crumbs sealed in, pile a generous amount of buttercream on to the top of the cake and work it down the sides using a small offset palette knife. It can be quite messy at this point.

10. For a rustic look, finish your cake by using your small offset palette knife to make short circular motions, scraping off any excess buttercream as you go.

11. For a smooth finish use a large offset palette knife held to the side of the cake at a 45-degree angle. Turn the cake while keeping your hand still and scrape off the excess buttercream as you go – wipe off your palette knife each time you bring it back in contact with the cake.

12. For the top, work from the sides into centre of the cake, scraping off the excess buttercream and cleaning your palette knife as you go. To make the finish really smooth, dip your palette knife into warm water, dry it off and smooth around the sides and top. Neaten up the plate that your cake is sitting on.

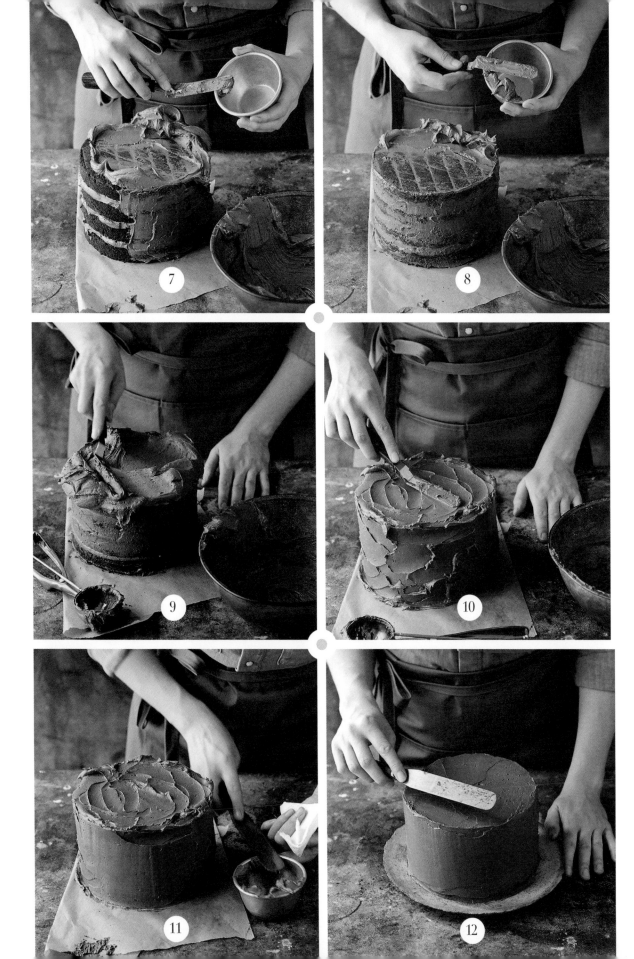

HOW TO FILL
A PIPING BAG

Filling a piping bag is a great skill to master. If you know how to use a piping bag you can achieve all kinds of decorating effects for cakes and make impressive meringues and choux pastry too. I prefer disposable bags with a metal icing tip and no coupler. Make sure that your buttercream or ganache is a smooth consistency before you start.

1. Using scissors, snip half the length of your icing tip off of the corner of the icing bag.

2. Place the icing tip inside the bag and make sure that the design at the end isn't blocked. If it is, remove the tip and snip a bit more off the end of your bag.

3. Turn the top of the bag inside out and place one hand inside the fold. Use a palette knife or rubber spatula to gradually fill the bag with buttercream. Don't fill more than halfway – this makes the bag much easier to handle and refill without getting too messy.

4. Push all of the buttercream down towards the icing tip, eliminating any pockets of air as you go. Twist the bag and grip between your thumb and forefinger. Keep twisting the bag until it's nice and taut and you can control the buttercream with just a small squeeze at the top.

HOW TO PIPE WITH BUTTERCREAM AND GANACHE

Piping with buttercream or ganache takes a bit of practice but will really make your cakes stand out. It's a good idea to practice on some baking parchment or back into the buttercream or ganache bowl before you pipe onto your cake. If you want to redo any of your piping, use an offset (angled) palette knife and a steady hand to carefully lift the piping off of the cake. Smooth over before re-piping.

Fill the piping bag (see page 134–5) and start squeezing from the top. You should only need to use your other hand for stability. Try to avoid handling the buttercream-filled part of the bag too much as you can warm up it up and make it lose its shape.

BEADED BORDER: To pipe beaded borders for the top and base of your cakes, angle an 8 mm ($^1/_3$ inch) plain tip at 45 degrees and start squeezing from the top of the bag to form a small ball of buttercream. Try to hover the tip just above the cake rather than touching the tip to the cake, to allow a nice shape to form. Stop squeezing as you gently move the tip along and squeeze again to form another ball that slightly overlaps and connects to the first one. Continue piping, trying to keep each ball the same size. It's easiest to do this using a cake turntable but if you don't have one, move the cake around as you work.

SMALL ROUNDS: To pipe small rounds for the top of your cake, angle the 8 mm ($^1/_3$ inch) plain tip at 90 degrees and about 5 mm ($^1/_4$ inch) about the surface of the cake. Start squeezing, letting a blob of buttercream form under the tip before you gently lift up and release the pressure to form the peak.

LARGE STAR ROUNDS: To pipe larger, equally spaced rounds, use an 18 mm ($^3/_4$ inch) large star tip and alternate between opposite sides of the cake to make them symmetrical. This technique works well with plain tips too.

ROPE BORDER: To pipe a rope border, use an 18 mm ($^3/_4$ inch) large star tip. Angle the tip at 45 degrees and make circular motions, applying pressure as you move upwards and releasing slightly as you move down and along.

BEADED BORDER

SMALL ROUNDS

LARGE STAR ROUNDS

ROPE BORDER

HOW TO CREATE A SWIRL EFFECT BUTTERCREAM FINISH

For a swirl-effect finish, start by covering your cake with a thick and smooth layer of buttercream. If you have a turntable, gently press the surface of buttercream with a clean palette knife held at a 45-degree angle and turn the cake, moving your hand slowly upwards as you turn. If you don't have a turntable, move your hand around the circumference of the cake slowly working your way from bottom to top. You can also make vertical strips with your palette knife starting from the bottom and finishing at the top.

HOW TO PIPE A SCALLOPED
BUTTERCREAM CAKE

This is such a pretty technique; it takes a bit of time but is easier than it looks. I prefer to use meringue-based buttercream as it requires quite a large batch to cover the whole cake and meringue-based buttercream has a lighter texture than regular buttercream.

1. Start with a crumb-coated, chilled cake (see pages 130–3). To build up the scalloped effect, pipe small rounds with your icing tip at a 90-degree angle, starting with a circle following the edge of the top of the cake (see page 137).

2. Each time you complete a circle of rounds on the top of the cake, or a line of rounds down the side of the cake, use a clean, dry palette knife to taper out each round from left to right. Continue piping, overlapping with the previous circle or line. Finish with a single round in the centre of the cake and lines of rounds down the side.

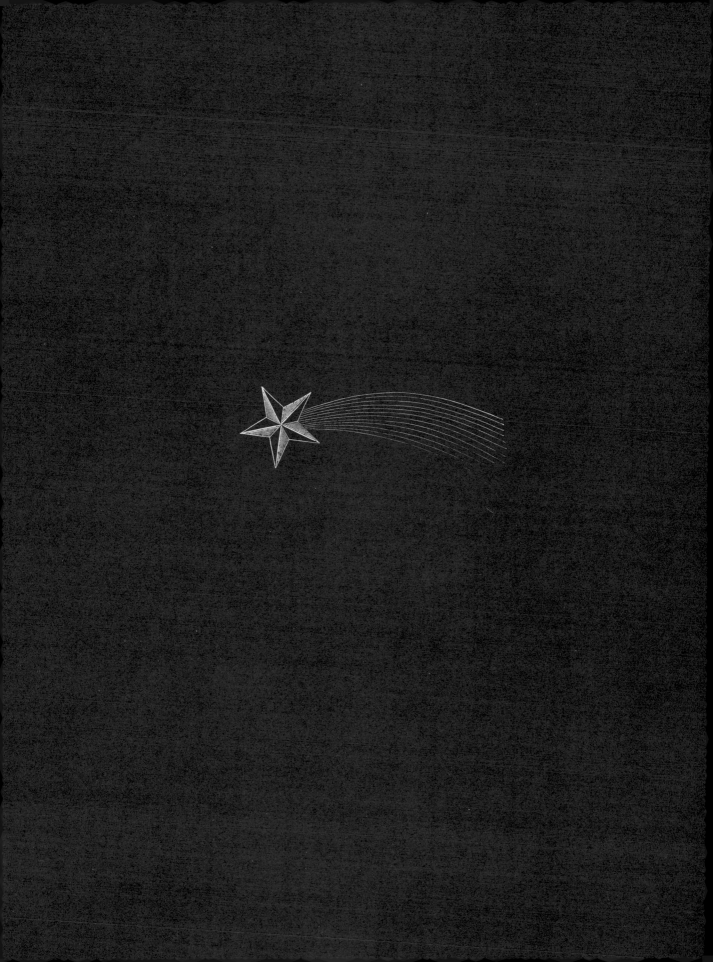

5

Final Touches

⊢————⊣

This chapter focuses on those final decorations that make a cake really special. From elegant cake flags and glamorous golden pecans to crystallised rosemary and fresh flowers. I've also included some tips on how to transport your cakes and how to photograph them.

CHOCOLATE CURLS

Chocolate curls are a cheap and easy decoration for chocolate-based cakes. I like to place them among a pile of berries on top of a cake or pile them up for some central height. The curls will keep for a week or two, so this is a great decoration to make ahead.

1. Start with a room temperature bar of dark or white chocolate flipped over with the squares facing downwards. Place some baking parchment on top of the chocolate and warm the surface up with the palm of your hand.

2. Use a sharp cookie cutter and drag it at an angle towards you. The curls should form inside the cutter. Vary the angle of the cutter until you find which one works best (the temperature and type of chocolate can affect how well your curls work).

3. Tip into a sealed container and transfer to the fridge to harden up before use. Avoid picking up the chocolate curls with your fingers as they can melt very easily.

CAKE FLAGS

Cake flags are a great way to add colour and height to your baked creations. For the Sea-Salted Caramel Chocolate Cake (see page 35) I've chosen turquoise and white ribbon. To make the flags, all you need are some wooden skewers or plastic lolly sticks, ribbon and a glue stick.

Dab some glue on the top of each skewer, wrap the ribbon around the stick and cut a 'V' shape into the end. Secure the 2 sides of the ribbon together with another dab of glue.

I also love making these from scraps of nice craft paper and once made a wedding cake topped with flags made from a vintage map print. If you're making paper flags you can customise them with handwritten messages or use rubber stamps and ink to decorate them.

HOW TO MAKE FONDANT CONFETTI SPRINKLES

This is an easy way to make your own sprinkles, and you can choose exactly the colour palette you want.
Colour fondant icing in whatever shades you like. I started with a ball of red and a ball of yellow fondant,
then I mixed the colours to create 2 shades of orange for a graduated palette.

1. Dust the work surface with icing sugar. Shape the fondant icing into little balls, all the same size.

2. Roll out the fondant balls side-by-side to a thickness of 2–3 mm (1/8 inch) to ensure that all of the sprinkles are the same size.

3. Cut out confetti shapes using an icing tip (I used an 8 mm/3/4 inch one). This is easier to do if you leave the rolled-out fondant to dry out for a few moments and dip your icing tip into some extra icing sugar first.

4. Set the fondant confetti on a surface dusted with icing sugar or some baking parchment for a few hours or overnight to harden. The confetti can be made ahead and stored in a sealed container at room temperature for several weeks.

TIP: Knead the fondant briefly to make it smooth before you roll it out. Fondant icing dries out so keep it covered with cling film (plastic wrap) as much as possible until you're ready to use it.

145

CRYSTALLISED ROSEMARY

Crystallised rosemary is really simple to make, and makes for a pretty decoration for rosemary-flavoured cakes

Follow the recipe for Rosemary Syrup (see page 83). You will also need 50 g (2 oz/¼ cup) caster (super-fine) sugar. Line a baking tray or plate with baking parchment. Dip the rosemary sprigs in the syrup and sprinkle all over with the sugar. Set aside to dry on the lined baking tray or plate for several hours or overnight.

PAINTING WITH EDIBLE GOLD LUSTRE DUST

Lustre dust is an edible powdered food colouring that comes in little pots or tubes. I love using it as a paint to give an intense shimmery gold colour to pecans, other nuts and fondant decorations. You can also use this technique to paint onto fondant-covered cakes.

1. Add a few drops of rejuvenator spirit or vodka to a small amount of lustre dust and mix with a paintbrush to form a smooth paste.

2. Place the pecans on a baking tray or some baking parchment and paint with the edible paint. Set aside to dry for a few minutes. If your paint dries out, just add a few more drops of alcohol.

HOW TO MAKE FRUIT SPARKLE WITH EDIBLE GLITTER

Edible glitter comes in lots of different colours but try to match the colour of your glitter to your fruit for maximum impact, otherwise it can look more grainy than sparkly. I've used black glitter for these blackberries.

1. Wash and dry your fruit, then set aside the prettiest and most evenly sized berries. Plan how many you'll need to decorate your cake.

2. Place a small amount of glitter on a little dish and dip the top of the berry in the glitter. A little goes a long way so you don't need much. Decorate your cake with the berries.

DECORATING CAKES WITH
FRESH FLOWERS

Fresh flowers are a beautiful and easy way of adding colour to your cake decoration. The important thing to remember is that they should be pesticide free (check with your florist or use wild or garden flowers that you know are safe). It's best to add your flowers just before you serve your cake as they will start to wilt once they're out of water. Remember to remove them before cutting and serving too.

• If you're making a cake for a special occasion like a wedding, let the florist know what size the cake is and ask them to arrange the flowers for you. They will be able help you choose flowers that will stay fresh out of water and will have clever tips for how to keep them looking their best.

• As an alternative, serve a simply decorated cake or a collection of cakes alongside arrangements of flowers in small jars, tins or vases.

HOW TO MAKE CRYSTALLISED ROSE PETALS

*This technique works with other edible flowers like violets and the yellow
primroses on my Lemon and Poppy Seed Syrup Cake (see page 30).
As with using fresh flowers, the important thing to remember is that your rose
petals should be pesticide free. I buy my edible flowers from a specialist supplier.*

1. Remove the petals from the flower head, trying to keep them in
one piece. Pick out the freshest looking petals.

2. Working in batches, brush a thin layer of egg white on to both
sides of each petal and sprinkle over the sugar to give each petal an
even coating.

3. Set aside on baking parchment or a wire rack to dry with a crisp
shell, uncovered, for several hours or overnight. Store at room
temperature and use within a day or so of making.

TRANSPORTING YOUR CAKES

Often, when I bake and decorate a cake it needs to travel before it can be eaten. After taking the time to make something special it's worth thinking about how to transport your creations so that they look just as good when they arrive at their destination.

• There are lots of tins and caddies available for storing cakes now but I prefer to keep a supply of cardboard cake boxes. These are cheap to buy online and from specialty shops, you don't need to remember to take them home at the end of the night and they come folded up so don't take up too much room in your kitchen.

• If you have a particularly tall cake to transport you can find extension panels to make the box taller. For tiered cakes, it's better to transport each tier individually and assemble the cake at the venue to avoid it toppling over en route.

• Consider adding decorations like berries and flowers at the last minute to keep them looking fresh.

• Use a cake board. You can either decorate and serve your cake directly on a board that fits snugly inside the cake box or you can decorate your cake on a board the same size as the cake, ready to be transferred to a cake stand or plate at your destination. It's a good idea to fix your cake to a second cake board that will fit snugly into the box using a small amount of buttercream to stop the cake from sliding around inside.

• Look out for flat bottomed patisserie-style bags to transport your cake boxes in, or tie some baker's twine or ribbon around the box like a parcel to keep it upright.

• Remember that you don't always need to make a huge cake to make a big impact. I love making mini tiered cakes and smaller cakes with four layers. They are also easier to transport.

• Take your own napkins, candles, matches and knife in case they're not easily available when you get to your destination.

PHOTOGRAPHING YOUR CAKES

When I've spent some time making a cake that I'm proud of, I love taking photos, whether it's with my DSLR camera to share on my blog or just a quick snap on my phone so that I can document what I've made. Either way, here are a few things that you should keep in mind to make your photos stand out and show off your creations looking their best.

• Natural light is best for photographing food. If there is some colour in your cake you could try adding a prop which picks out the colour say, a raspberry cake with a deep pink napkin or a few lemons for a lemon cake. I also love using a simple piece of crumpled baking parchment under baked things in photos.

• Try experimenting with different angles. Does the top of your cake have some beautiful piping or artfully placed sprinkles? Try showing it off with an overhead shot. Imagine you're about to serve your cake and think about the angle that you would naturally see it from if you were sitting at a table. Maybe there's a knife or a stack of plates nearby? Or maybe you've just finished sprinkling some icing sugar on to the cake and there's a bit left on the table? It's nice to tell a bit of a story in your photos sometimes.

• If in doubt, keep it simple and have fun getting inspired by other photos that you like.

APRIL CARTER

├────────┤

Author of *trEATs* and the baking blog *Rhubarb & Rose*, April Carter loves making delicious and beautifully decorated cakes. She trained at Leiths School of Food & Wine and lives in London. *Decorated* is her third book.

ACKNOWLEDGEMENTS

├────────┤

It's been so much fun writing this book and there are lots of people that have worked together to make it happen.

Special thanks to Kate Pollard, Kajal Mistry, Jennifer Seymour, Emma Marijewycz, Laura Nickoll, Stephen King and the team at Hardie Grant.

To Danielle Wood for the beautiful photos and for being so great to work with. Thanks to Ted for keeping us going in the studio.

To Ami Smithson, thank you for the wonderful design.

To Livia Brockhaus, a special thank you for the many hours of cake baking, decorating and tasting and to Natalie Haywood, Katie Marshall and Jack Reed for their excellent assisting and careful recipe testing.

To all of my friends at Leiths, especially Heli, Liv, Nat, Ben, Dan, Jess and Alice, who tested recipes, ate cakes and generally made this a brilliant year, thank you!

To my friends and family, my mum Liz and my brother Jack, thank you for always supporting me and being excited about my various projects.

Alex, thank you for everything.

Stockists

CAKE DECORATING SUPPLIES, CAKE BOARDS AND BOXES

UK
www.cakescookiesandcraftsshop.co.uk

AUSTRALIA
www.bakingpleasures.com.au
www.cakedecoratingsolutions.com.au
www.creativegiftpackaging.com

US
www.cooksdream.com
www.sweetwise.com
www.brpboxshop.com

MOULDS AND CAKE TINS

UK
www.divertimenti.co.uk
www.lakeland.co.uk
www.invictabakeware.co.uk

AUSTRALIA
www.cakesaroundtown.com.au
www.kitchenwaredirect.com.au

US
www.macys.com
www.specialtybottle.com

FLAVOURINGS AND CRYSTALLISED PETALS

UK
www.souschef.co.uk
www.uncleroys.co.uk

AUSTRALIA
bakingpleasures.com.au

US
www.herbspro.com
www.marxfoods.com

CAKE STANDS

UK
www.re-foundobjects.com
www.johnlewis.com

AUSTRALIA
www.cakesaroundtown.com.au
www.kitchenwaredirect.com.au

US
cooksdream.com

RIBBON AND CRAFT PAPER

UK
www.paperchase.co.uk
www.liberty.co.uk

AUSTRALIA
www.kikki-k.com
www.shop.cottonon.com/typoshop
www.spotlight.com.au

US
www.hobbylobby.com
www.michaels.com
www.paper-source.com

FLOWERS

UK
www.scarletandviolet.com

EDIBLE FLOWERS

UK
www.eatmyflowers.co.uk

INDEX

DECORATED

BY APRIL CARTER

First published in 2014 by Hardie Grant Books

Hardie Grant Books (UK)
5th & 6th Floor
52–53 Southwark Street
London SE1 1RU

www.hardiegrant.co.uk

Hardie Grant Books (Australia)
Ground Floor, Building 1
658 Church Street Melbourne,
VIC 3121
www.hardiegrant.com.au

British Library Cataloguing-in-Publication Data. A catalogue record for this book is available from the British Library.

ISBN 978-174270-772-3

Publisher: Kate Pollard
Senior Editor: Kajal Mistry
Contributing Editors: Laura Nickoll and Susan Pegg
Cover and Internal Design: Ami Smithson
Photographer © Danielle Wood

Colour Reproduction by p2d

Find this book on Cooked.
Cooked.com.au
Cooked.co.uk

Printed and bound in China by 1010

10 9 8 7 6 5 4 3 2 1